THE ROASTING TRAY COOKBOOK

THE ROASTING TRAY
COOKBOOK

101 recipes for simple and nutritious meals straight from the oven

JENNY TSCHIESCHE

Photography by Steve Painter

RYLAND PETERS & SMALL
LONDON • NEW YORK

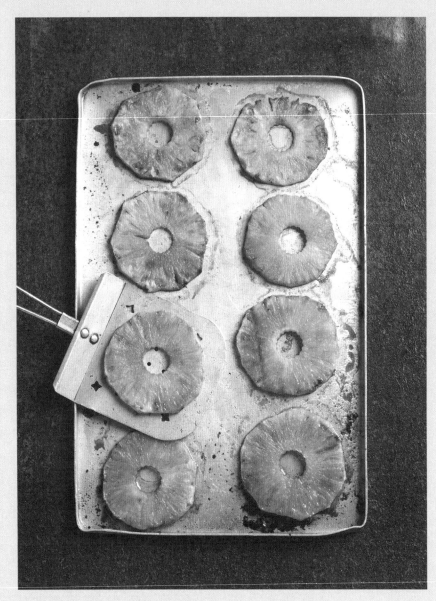

First published in 2018 by
Ryland Peters & Small
20–21 Jockey's Fields, London
WC1R 4BW
and 341 E 116th St, New York NY 10029
www.rylandpeters.com

10 9 8 7 6 5 4 3 2

ISBN: 978-1-78879-060-4

Printed in China

Notes:
• Both British (Metric) and American
(Imperial plus US cups) measurements
are included in these recipes for your
convenience, however it is important to work
with one set of measurements only and not
alternate between the two within a recipe.
• All spoon measurements are level unless
otherwise specified. A teaspoon is 5 ml,
a tablespoon is 15 ml.
• All eggs are medium (UK) or large (US),
unless specified as large, in which case
US extra-large should be used. Uncooked
or partially cooked eggs should not be
served to the very old, frail, young children,
pregnant women or those with compromised
immune systems.
• Ovens should be preheated to the
specified temperatures. We recommend
using an oven thermometer. If using a
fan-assisted oven, adjust temperatures
according to the manufacturer's instructions.

*To Werner, Amalie and Samuel,
thank you for the loan of your
tastebuds and for your critiquing
skills but most of all thanks for being
so very supportive throughout the
process of creating this book.*

Senior designer Toni Kay
Editor Miriam Catley
Head of production
  Patricia Harrington
Art director Leslie Harrington
Editorial director Julia Charles
Publisher Cindy Richards

Photography & prop styling
  Steve Painter
Food stylist Lucy McKelvie
Indexer Vanessa Bird

CONTENTS

INTRODUCTION

Modern life is busy, chaotic, and full on. Sometimes getting dinner on the table seems like the hardest thing to do after a long day, let alone trying to think up something nutritious everyone will like. It is surprising, therefore, that out of all the modern gadgets in our kitchens designed to make our lives easier, the greatest piece of equipment of them all turns out to be the simplest; the sheet pan, also known as the baking tray or roasting tin. As you will find out in this book, you barely need anything else, apart from a knife or two and (occasionally) a frying pan/skillet.

Above all, this book is for families, particularly those parents who want to ensure that the next generation grow up with a real food culture, not a processed food culture. I'm a nutritionist who works away from home, running workshops or in clinic, and this one pan way of cooking has, on so many occasions, saved me from the edge of madness. It's one of those methods that really requires very little thought and, importantly, little skill. While I am a recipe developer, I am not a chef so you won't find you're being expected to use any fancy culinary skills in this book. What you will find is simple recipes that are achievable by all.

I spent several years studying for a nutrition degree at the Institute of Optimum Nutrition while raising a family, and learnt the hard way that family life and healthy eating do not always go hand in hand. Once I graduated, I set about advising groups of parents, young athletes and those in the corporate environment on well-being and optimal nutrition through workshops and in my nutrition clinic. As time went by I realized that whilst theory is a good thing, practical advice is even better. The practical advice that spoke loudest and reaped the greatest benefits seemed to be in the form of simple recipes.

What started out as developing recipes for my workshops and clients grew in an unexpected direction. I was soon developing recipes for major health campaigns run by the BBC and Cancer Research to name a few as well as for many large brands of kitchenware. It's something I have developed a real passion for and simply love to do. I've worked in schools, for sports organisations and individuals and one of the things that makes me most excited is working with families to make healthy eating easier, whether it is making lunchboxes more interesting or dinner times less stressful.

Each recipe or recipe combination in this book aims to present the opportunity to consume multiple vegetables as well as the right balance of other food groups. In particular I include the right kinds of fats, i.e. those our body knows how to break down and metabolize, and the right kinds of protein from identifiable sources and in an unadulterated and unprocessed (other than cheese, of course) form. The simplicity of a meal that combines some protein, some fat and some carbohydrate, all in an unprocessed form is something our bodies will thank us for both now and in years to come. It's a way of eating we were designed to benefit from. Whilst some are lighter meals others are full-on family feasts, and some are even dinner-party worthy. I've also made suggestions regarding which recipes might work well alongside one another.

Way back when man discovered fire and the benefits provided by fire, the culinary possibilities exploded and we really started thriving and surviving as a species. Nowadays, we are not thriving so much, and you could argue we are not surviving either. More like hanging on by our fingernails. Some experts believe this current generation of children may not outlive their parents and that's largely due to the environment in which children are growing up. One of the issues with modern living is the abundance of processed junk food. This book aims to show you just how easy and how simple a step it is to take to create colourful, diverse tray bakes. These are the sorts of meals that the whole family will enjoy, making it possible to sit down together for a meal. If that's not a possibility due to your varied time schedules then simply leave some portions on low in the oven for later; or save the leftovers from the night before and serve these up the following day in lunchboxes or as an earlier evening meal for younger children.

One piece of advice is this; do not get stressed about providing foods that your children will eat every meal. Even when they do refuse to eat something remember that so long as they are exposed to that foodstuff regularly it won't become an issue. Just don't force them to eat it. With cooking on a sheet pan children can also get involved as it is such a simple method of cooking. Experience and scientific studies tell us that those who are involved in the process of creating a meal are far more likely to consume that meal too.

This book will show you that real food meals are not rocket science. They are not complicated and they don't take a huge amount of your time. It's about making the oven do the work. As you gain confidence with this method of cooking you'll find there are so many possibilities and with each you'll free up more of your valuable time. There's now no need to compromise.

Real food ingredients are the very basis of healthy eating. Creating recipes that combine real food ingredients in a nutritionally balanced way has been a pleasure and a joy. I hope that you too can gain from the simplicity of the recipes shared as part of this book.

STORECUPBOARD EXPLANATIONS

Stevia powder This is a natural sweetener that is known to have a glycaemic index of zero. What that means is that it doesn't raise your blood sugar levels when you eat it. However, when purchasing stevia powder be clear in what you are looking for. You want as pure as possible without added artificial sweeteners. Buying the powder in a pure form means you can use tiny amounts in place of larger amounts of sugar because it is so sweet. So for example, 200 g/1 cup sugar is equivalent to about ½ teaspoon stevia.

Coconut sugar This is a natural sugar made from the sap of the coconut tree. Unlike white, refined sugar, it is known to retain quite a few nutrients found in the coconut palm. The Philippine Department of Agriculture measured the glycaemic index of coconut sugar as 35. This is much lower than table sugar, which is somewhere around 65.

Garlic powder This is dehydrated ground garlic and it gives the flavour but not texture of fresh garlic to a dish.

Onion powder This is made from dehydrated onions that have been ground into a powder. Of course you will get great flavour from this condiment.

Mustard powder This is made from grinding mustard seeds. It's not as pungent as the jars of mustard we use with cooked meat. It's a fantastic flavour provider though, especially in marinades and burgers.

Tamari or coconut aminos Soy sauce is made to varying standards and sometimes with unwanted additives. Buying tamari, which is a gluten-free version of soy sauce, is often a good way to buy purer soy sauce. If you want a soy-free version, then coconut aminos are recommended.

Tempeh This is a fermented soy food. Fermented foods in general are very good for our gut health as they help to populate the gut with better bacteria.

Miso This is another fermented soy product that not only provides beneficial bacteria for the gut but also gives dishes a satisfying 'umami' taste.

Kefir/Greek yogurt Both kefir and good quality Greek yogurt contain probiotic bacteria which have been shown to improve the populations of good bacteria in the gut. This in turn can provide a boost to the immune system. Kefir can be purchased from health food stores or Polish supermarkets.

Coconut milk yogurt For those who want a creamy, dairy-free alternative to yogurt, there's a range of non-dairy coconut milk-based yogurts now on the market.

Ghee This is butter that has had the moisture, proteins and sugars removed. It therefore doesn't burn. It's also a source of Vitamins A, D and K2 fats.

Coconut oil The structure of coconut oil, being primarily Medium Chain Triglycerides (other saturated fats are mostly Long Chain), means it is very easily digested.

Balsamic glaze This glaze should be made from a combination of cooked grape must and balsamic vinegar, which creates a mellower and less tart flavour than balsamic vinegar on its own.

Plantains Although part of the banana family they do need cooking before eating. Ripe plantain is used in a variety of dishes, both savoury and sweet. In this book I've used fresh ripe plantain as a dessert and fried plantain chips as a gluten-free crispy coating for chicken nuggets.

EQUIPMENT EXPLANATIONS

Baking multiple whole meals on sheet pans calls for at least two different-sized pans. In the course of writing this book I have trialled a lot of different sheet pans. I would say my favourites have been stoneware, stainless steel or silicone for ease of use and taste reasons. I am sure you will have an inclination about which you might prefer, but if you don't and are just starting out, the stainless steel is probably the most cost-effective place to start.

The sizes I tend to use are a small dish, such as a loaf pan, 450 g/1 lb. or 900 g/2 lb. in capacity, a 20 x 20 cm/8 x 8 in. sheet pan and a large roasting pan. Of course some implements such as spatulas, fish slices and wooden spoons have also been essential, as have adjustable measuring spoons to help get the balance of spices, herbs and other additions right.

I love having a food processor handy for making dishes even more quickly, especially sauces for some of the saucier tray bakes. Being able to finely chop onions, garlic and herbs, for example, in a food processor makes the whole process that much less hassle. That doesn't mean you have to make a large investment (or any at all if you are handy with a knife and can cut things fine, unlike me) as even a manual food processor can help speed things up a little.

This book will open up a range of possibilities as far as roasting vegetables go, and to that end will make some vegetables far more appealing to some, let's say limited palates, than they have been previously.

WHAT VEGETABLES TO ROAST?

When you mention 'roast vegetables' to people they tend to respond with 'oh yes, we love roasted Mediterranean veg in our household' or indeed 'we love roast potatoes with our Sunday lunch'. However, you can roast so many more vegetables than either of these two common examples allow for. If you're not sure if a particular vegetable can be roasted, my recommendation is to just give it a try. It might not end up being your favourite way to eat that vegetable, but it's definitely worth the experiment to find out.

A Good dose of good fat Toss your chopped vegetables in sufficient oil to coat evenly. Ideal oils include olive oils, ghee, butter (melted) or coconut oil. One sheet pan may need 1–2 tablespoons oil/fat.

The exception to this is aubergine/eggplant where you'll need up to 3 tablespoons oil for a large aubergine/eggplant because they absorb so much of the oil, but then that's part of their appeal. The oil/fat greatly improves the cooking and flavour.

Add some seasoning Most vegetables benefit from the addition of sea salt and often some pepper too. You can also add other flavoursome seasoning such as vinegar, spices and herbs to really make the flavours come alive.

Choose the sheet pan carefully In order that the vegetables cook evenly there should be a bit of space in the pan you're baking them in. For this reason it's good to have more than one sheet pan available to you at any one time. If the vegetables are too crowded they tend to steam rather than bake. That's not the texture nor the taste that you're looking for.

Preheat the oven Make sure your oven is hot before you put the vegetables in. I like to roast my vegetables at 200°C (400°F) Gas 6. There are exceptions to this. For example roasted potatoes are better and crispier at hotter temperatures.

When are they cooked? The cooked vegetables should be tender when a fork is poked into them. They may also be some charred bits on the edges.

General roasting times for vegetables
Cooking times are for roasting vegetables at 200°C (400°F) Gas 6.
Root vegetables: 35–45 minutes, depending on how small you cut them.
Cruciferous vegetables: 15–25 minutes, depending on how small you cut them.
Green Vegetables and Nightshades: 10–30 minutes, depending on how you cut them.
Onions: 30–45 minutes, depending on how crispy you like them and how you cut them.

VEGETABLES YOU CAN ROAST		HEALTH FACTS	DELICIOUS ADDITIONS
Greens	Asparagus, courgette/zucchini, kale	Low carbohydrate. Low calorie. Nutrient dense – providing vitamin C, vitamin K and vitamin A.	Garlic salt, lemon juice, pesto/basil, salt, pepper
Root vegetables	Potatoes, beetroot/beet, pumpkin, sweet potato, white sweet potato, parsnip, swede/rutabaga, celeriac, butternut squash, carrots	Being root veg, they absorb lots of nutrients from the soil. Rich in vitamin C, B vitamins and beta-carotene. Slow-burning carbohydrate source. A source of fibre.	Balsamic vinegar, garlic, salt, pepper
Cruciferous vegetables	Broccoli, Brussels sprouts, cauliflower, cabbage	Contains antioxidants (particularly beta carotene and the compound sulforaphane). High in fibre, vitamins and minerals. Contain indole-3-carbidol (I3C) which changes the way oestrogen is metabolized and may prevent hormone based cancers. Contain a phytochemical known as isothiocyanates, which stimulate our bodies to break down potential carcinogens.	Spices – dried turmeric, cumin, dried chilli/hot pepper flakes, black onion seeds, bacon
Nightshades	Potatoes, tomatoes, (bell) peppers, aubergine/eggplant	A source of antioxidants, Vitamin C and beta-carotene.	Oregano, marjoram, cheese such as mozzarella or goats' cheese
Onion family	Onion, red onion, shallots, garlic, leeks	Linked to health improvements as far ranging as improving cholesterol levels, wound healing and clearing up infection. A powerhouse of minerals and vitamins.	Balsamic vinegar, thyme, mustard
Mushrooms		Generally Asian mushrooms provide the greatest health benefits. Mushrooms do provide an 'umami' effect which makes a meal containing mushrooms more satisfying and may lead to reduced food intake overall.	Garlic, thyme, parsley, pesto

MEAT

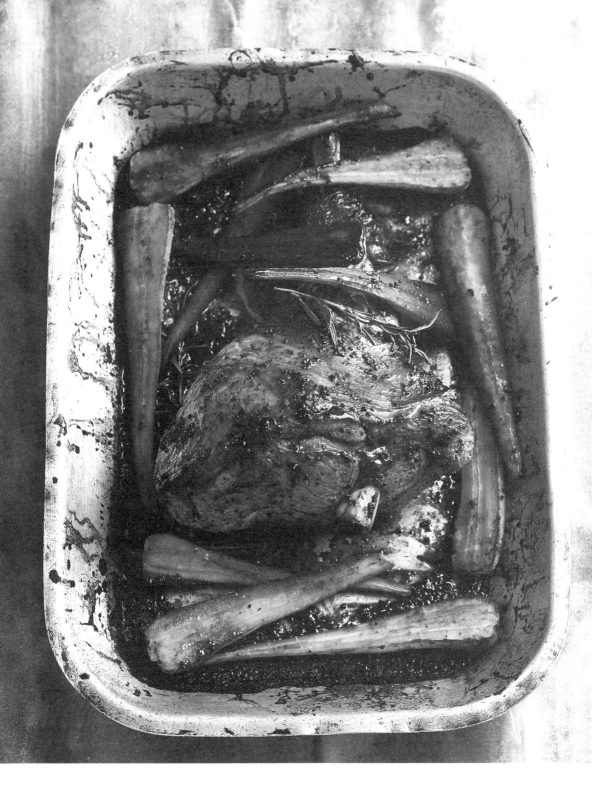

ALL-IN-ONE BREAKFAST

You'll need just five ingredients for this simple one pan dish. It's a delicious twist on the traditional breakfast of bacon and eggs and so quick to prepare you'll make it all the time.

4 large field mushrooms
2 tablespoons olive oil
12 slices Parma ham/prosciutto or bresaola
4 eggs
1 tablespoon freshly chopped parsley
sea salt and freshly ground black pepper

SERVES 2

Preheat the oven to 220°C (425°F) Gas 7.

Place the mushrooms on a sheet pan with sides. Drizzle over the olive oil and season with salt and pepper.

Bake in the preheated oven for 15 minutes. Check that the mushrooms are almost cooked through. If not, cook for up to a further 5 minutes.

Add the ham or bresaola to the sheet pan and crack the eggs on top.

Bake for another 7–10 minutes until the eggs are just cooked.

Remove from the oven, sprinkle over the fresh parsley and enjoy.

BREAKFAST SLICE

Who says breakfast food even exists? There are cultures where there is no such thing as breakfast food. Food is food and can be eaten at any meal. We often consider eggs to be predominantly a breakfast food so I've named this Breakfast Slice, but honestly, you could enjoy it any time of day.

6 eggs
2 medium courgettes/zucchini, grated
2 medium carrots, grated
2 onions, grated
5 slices unsmoked back bacon,
    finely chopped
1½ teaspoons dried mixed herbs
55 g/¼ cup ghee, plus a little more
    for greasing the pan
55 g/⅓ cup coconut flour
½ teaspoon sea salt
pinch of freshly ground black pepper

20 x 25-cm/8 x 10-in. sheet pan with sides,
    greased

SERVES 2-3

Preheat the oven to 200°C (400°F) Gas 6.

Whisk the eggs in a bowl until they are light and fluffy.

In a large bowl, mix together the eggs, grated vegetables, bacon, herbs, ghee, flour and seasoning.

Pour the mixture into the prepared sheet pan. Bake in the preheated oven for 45 minutes or until the top is golden brown and a fork inserted into the middle comes out clean. Serve immediately.

Serving Suggestion: Serve with baked mushrooms and sliced avocado.

BAKED EGGS WITH CHORIZO, TOMATO & SPINACH

A delicious mix of spicy chorizo and tangy tomatoes, combined with protein-rich eggs. A feast for the eyes, full of naturally colourful ingredients, this will be a filling dinner winner!

160 g/5^3/$_4$ oz. frozen spinach (defrosted, excess liquid removed by squeezing through a sieve/strainer and roughly torn)

4 tablespoons chorizo sausage, roughly chopped

300 g/10^1/$_2$ oz. passata/strained tomatoes

^{3}/$_4$ teaspoon sea salt

4 eggs

a handful of fresh baby spinach leaves (optional)

SERVES 2

Preheat the oven to 220°C (425°F) Gas 7.

Place the spinach, chorizo and passata/strained tomatoes in a small sheet pan with sides with the salt and stir to combine. Make four small wells in the mixture and break in the eggs.

Bake in the preheated oven for 25 minutes or until the egg whites are cooked. Serve immediately.

Serving Suggestion: Add fresh baby spinach leaves just before serving to wilt gently over the dish.

SWEET POTATO & KALE HASH WITH BAKED EGGS

Bacon and eggs combine with the 'powerhouse' flavours of sun-dried tomatoes and sweet potato and the super green leafy vegetable, kale, to create a delicious hash.

2 medium sweet potatoes (approx. 500 g/1 lb. 2 oz.), peeled and grated

65 g/^{3}/$_4$ cup baby kale leaves or the same amount of kale, destalked and chopped

6 slices unsmoked back bacon, thinly sliced

1^1/$_2$ tablespoons dried oregano

90 g/^{1}/$_2$ cup sun-dried tomato pesto or sun-dried tomato paste

1 tablespoon olive oil

6 eggs

SERVES 2-4

Preheat the oven to 200°C (400°F) Gas 6.

Mix the sweet potato with the kale, bacon, oregano, pesto/paste and olive oil. Place the mixture into a sheet pan with sides and bake in the preheated oven for 15 minutes.

Make six holes in the mixture and crack in the eggs. Bake for a further 7–10 minutes until the eggs are just cooked. Serve.

HONEY & MUSTARD SAUSAGE BAKE

Ah, honey and mustard, a classic flavour combination and one we have loved for years as a family. When I knew I would be creating an oven-based recipe book this combination with sausages immediately came to mind. This dish is one of those classics that gets made again and again and again.

3 red onions, cut into thin wedges
3 medium sweet potatoes, peeled and cut lengthways, then into 1-cm/½-in. semi-circles
300 g/10½ oz. asparagus, washed and trimmed
10 chestnut mushrooms, wiped clean
2 tablespoons olive oil
1 teaspoon sea salt
2 tablespoons wholegrain mustard
2 tablespoons honey
24 chipolatas

SERVES 6

Preheat the oven to 200°C (400°F) Gas 6.

Combine the vegetables in a large sheet pan with sides with the olive oil and salt and bake in the preheated oven for 10 minutes.

Meanwhile, combine the mustard and honey in a large bowl and stir in the sausages, leaving them to marinate for 10 minutes or so.

Add the sausages and the marinade to the sheet pan and give everything a good stir.

Bake for a further 25 minutes until the sausages are cooked through. Serve.

PORK MEATBALLS WITH SPROUTS & SWEET POTATO

Brussels sprouts – love them or hate them? Hopefully this combination will persuade you that they really are a welcome addition to some dishes. Trust me!

1 large onion, finely chopped
2 teaspoons garlic salt
1 kg/2¼ lb. minced/ground pork
½ teaspoon ground mace
½ teaspoon dried thyme
⅛ teaspoon white pepper
500 g/1 lb. 2 oz. Brussels sprouts, trimmed
3 small sweet potatoes (approx. 500 g/1 lb. 2 oz. peeled weight), peeled and cut into 2-cm/¾-in. cubes
4 tablespoons olive oil
½ teaspoon sea salt
3 garlic cloves, crushed
fresh thyme, to serve

SERVES 4

Preheat the oven to 200°C (400°F) Gas 6.

In a large bowl, mix together the onion, garlic salt, pork, ground mace, dried thyme and white pepper. Roll into table tennis-sized meatballs. Set aside.

Toss the sprouts and sweet potatoes in the olive oil, sprinkle over the salt and stir in the crushed garlic.

Put the vegetables on a large sheet pan with sides and bake in the preheated oven for 20 minutes.

Add the meatballs to the sheet pan, then bake for a further 25 minutes until the meatballs are cooked through. Serve with fresh thyme leaves scattered over the dish.

SAUSAGE, CELERY & TOMATO BAKE

Clean-tasting celery and the sharp and sweet flavours of the tomatoes combine brilliantly with the salty sausages.

4 celery stalks, thickly sliced
   on the diagonal about
   2 cm/³/₄ in. each in length
1 red onion, quartered
2 garlic cloves, peeled
¹/₂ teaspoon sea salt
¹/₂ teaspoon freshly ground
   black pepper

1 tablespoon olive oil
4 large tomatoes (not beef
   tomatoes), cut into quarters
1 teaspoon fennel seeds
10 thick good-quality sausages

SERVES 4

Preheat the oven to 200°C (400°F) Gas 6.

In a large bowl, mix together the celery, onion, garlic, salt, pepper and olive oil. Put the vegetables on a sheet pan with sides and lay the tomato quarters on the outside edges of the pan. Sprinkle over the fennel seeds. Lay the sausages on top of the vegetables but not the tomatoes.

Bake in the preheated oven for 55 minutes. Turn the sausages and the vegetables once during baking. Serve.

Serving Suggestion: Serve with baked sweet potatoes.

JERK PINEAPPLE PORK LOIN

1¹/₄ teaspoons sea salt
2 tablespoons jerk seasoning
500-g/1 lb. 2 oz. pork fillet
227-g/8-oz. can pineapple rings, drained
   (keep the juice)
300 g/10¹/₂ oz. new potatoes,
   chopped into 1-cm/¹/₂-in. pieces
1 teaspoon olive oil
100 g/3¹/₂ oz. white cabbage, thickly sliced
1 tablespoon ghee or coconut oil

SERVES 4

Pork and pineapple go together so well. This is taste of the Caribbean in a dish. It tastes great accompanied by the Creamy Coleslaw (page 122).

Mix 1 teaspoon salt and the jerk seasoning together in a bowl. Cut the pork fillet in half and roll each half in the salt/spice mix. Drizzle a tablespoon of pineapple juice over each half fillet, cover and leave in the refrigerator to marinate for 5–8 hours ideally.

When you're ready to cook, preheat the oven to 200°C (400°F) Gas 6.

Put the potatoes on a sheet pan with sides. Add the cabbage to the sheet pan, then drizzle over the olive oil and sprinkle over the salt.

Heat the ghee or coconut oil in a frying pan/skillet. Add the pork fillets and sear each side briefly. Wrap each half fillet in foil and place on the same sheet pan as the potatoes. Bake in the preheated oven for 25 minutes until cooked.

Slice the pork and return to the pan. Pour any juices from their foil packages into the pan. Stir the slices with the vegetables plus another 2 tablespoons of the pineapple juice. Place back into the oven for just 1 minute to heat the sauce through. Serve with a pineapple ring on each plate.

CROWD-PLEASER MEATLOAF & GARLIC BROCCOLI

What's not to love about a meatloaf? This one can certainly feed a family!
It's packed full of hidden vegetables too. That's a win win!

8 slices unsmoked back bacon
2 carrots, roughly chopped
2 celery stalks, roughly chopped
1 onion, roughly chopped
2 garlic cloves, peeled
3 tablespoons freshly chopped parsley
800 g/1¾ lb. minced/ground beef
2 eggs
40 g/⅓ cup ground flaxseeds/linseeds
65 ml/¼ cup milk
1½ tablespoons butter/ghee/coconut oil
2 teaspoons sea salt
½ teaspoon freshly ground black pepper
1 head of broccoli, cut into florets
2 medium courgettes/zucchini,
    cut into 2-cm/¾-in. slices
1 teaspoon garlic salt
2 teaspoons olive oil
3 tablespoons BBQ Sauce (no added sugar),
    such as Dr Will's, or balsamic glaze

33 x 22 x 10-cm/13 x 8½ x 4-in. loaf pan

SERVES 4-6

Preheat the oven to 200°C (400°F) Gas 6.

Lay four slices of the bacon in the base of the loaf pan.

Put the carrots, celery, onion, garlic and parsley in a food processor and finely chop. Remove from the food processor and put in a bowl. Mix in the minced/ground beef, eggs, flaxseeds/linseeds, milk and butter/ghee/coconut oil as well as the seasoning until thoroughly combined.

Push the meat mixture into the loaf pan on top of the bacon and top the mixture with the remaining bacon slices, tucking the ends down the sides of the loaf pan.

Bake in the preheated oven for 25 minutes.

Meanwhile, put the remaining prepared vegetables onto a sheet pan with high sides, sprinkle over the garlic salt and drizzle over the olive oil.

Once 25 minutes is up, coat the top of the meatloaf with the BBQ sauce or balsamic glaze.

At this stage, put the vegetables into the oven and bake both the meatloaf and the vegetables for a further 25 minutes. Toss the vegetables once during cooking.

Serve the meatloaf and the baked vegetables together.

BEEF & CHORIZO MEATBALLS IN MEDITERRANEAN SAUCE WITH PEPPERS

Moist Spanish meatballs made from beef and chorizo combine with sweet peppers to create a scrumptious all-in-one meal.

1 medium red (bell) pepper, deseeded and cut into 1-cm/1/2-in. strips
1 medium orange (bell) pepper, deseeded and cut into 1-cm/1/2-in. strips
1/2 teaspoon sea salt
2 teaspoons olive oil
1 onion, finely chopped
1 garlic clove, finely chopped
500 g/1 lb. 2 oz. passata/ strained tomatoes
1 teaspoon dried marjoram or oregano
1 tablespoon tomato purée/paste
1 teaspoon garlic salt
1/2 teaspoon honey
100 g/31/2 oz. chorizo
400 g/14 oz. minced/ ground beef

SERVES 4

Preheat the oven to 200°C (400°F) Gas 6.

Put the (bell) peppers on a sheet pan with high sides, sprinkle over the salt and drizzle over the olive oil. Bake in the preheated oven for 15 minutes.

Meanwhile, put the onion, garlic, passata/strained tomatoes, marjoram/oregano, tomato purée/paste, garlic salt and honey in a bowl and stir together to make a sauce.

To make the meatballs, finely chop the chorizo or use a food processor to grind it to a paste and mix it together with the minced/ground beef. Roll the minced meat mix into 12 evenly-sized meatballs.

After 15 minutes of cooking the (bell) peppers, add the sauce and the meatballs to the sheet pan. Cover with foil and bake for a further 25–30 minutes until the meatballs are just cooked and still moist. Serve.

ROOT VEG & CORNED BEEF HASH

The taste of my 1980s childhood but with a healthier twist. Still the familiar taste of corned beef, but now combined with root vegetables in place of the traditional potatoes, giving this a boost of nutrients.

500 g/1 lb. 2 oz. mixed root vegetables, coarsely chopped in a food processor (to about 1-cm/3/8-in. pieces)
3 small red onions, quartered
1 tablespoon Worcestershire sauce
1 teaspoon wholegrain mustard
1 tablespoon freshly chopped mixed herbs
3 tablespoons coconut oil or ghee
4 eggs
1 x 340-g/12-oz. can reduced-salt corned beef, cut into 2-cm/1-in. cubes

SERVES 4

Preheat the oven to 200°C (400°F) Gas 6.

In a large bowl, mix together the vegetables, Worcestershire sauce, mustard, herbs and coconut oil or ghee.

Spread the coated vegetables out on a sheet pan with sides. Bake in the preheated oven for 25 minutes.

Remove from the oven, make four wells in the vegetables and crack in the eggs. Add the corned beef and bake for a further 6–9 minutes or until the eggs are cooked. Serve immediately.

STEAK BURGERS WITH BALSAMIC ROAST VEGETABLES

OK, this is a bit of a cheat meal because someone has already made the steak burgers for you, but this quick-win midweek meal will be very well received.

2 onions, cut into eighths
2 courgettes/zucchini, cut into 2-cm/3/4-in. thick semi-circles
6–8 mushrooms, cut into quarters
1 head of broccoli, cut into florets
2 tablespoons olive oil
1 1/2 tablespoons balsamic glaze
3/4 teaspoon sea salt
8 steak burgers

SERVES 4

Preheat the oven to 200°C (400°F) Gas 6.

In a large bowl, mix the vegetables, olive oil, balsamic glaze and salt together.

Put the vegetables on a sheet pan with sides and the steak burgers on a separate sheet pan. Bake both sheet pans in the preheated oven for 25 minutes or until both the vegetables and burgers are cooked. Serve.

Serving Suggestion: Add a dash of chilli/hot red pepper sauce for some heat.

ROASTED ROQUEFORT BURGERS WITH GARLIC BROCCOLI

The key to making these burgers moist and succulent is ensuring they're moulded into flat patties and getting the cooking time right. If you are not keen on blue cheese simply add your favourite cheese topping or go without the cheese. These burgers work well with crispy cooked broccoli.

800 g/1 3/4 lb. minced/ground beef
1 teaspoon sea salt
1 teaspoon dried thyme
1 teaspoon mustard powder
1 egg
2 teaspoons Worcestershire sauce
1/2 teaspoon freshly ground black pepper
1 large head of broccoli, cut into very small florets
1 tablespoon olive oil
1/2 teaspoon garlic salt
1 x vine of cherry tomatoes (with about 12 cherry tomatoes on the vine)
40 g/1/3 cup Roquefort cheese, crumbled

SERVES 4

Preheat the oven to 200°C (400°F) Gas 6.

In a large bowl, mix together the beef, salt, thyme, mustard powder, egg, Worcestershire sauce and pepper. Mix really well with your hands to ensure all of the seasonings are evenly distributed. Shape the mixture into eight equal burgers. Press the burgers flat to ensure even baking.

Put the broccoli on a sheet pan with sides and sprinkle over the olive oil and garlic salt. Lay the burgers on a wire rack in the preheated oven with another sheet pan below to catch the fat as it drips through.

Bake the burgers and the broccoli in the preheated oven for about 15–17 minutes. Turn the burgers after 5 minutes baking time. Add the vine tomatoes to the broccoli sheet pan 10 minutes before the end of cooking.

Once cooked, crumble the Roquefort over each burger. Serve the burgers, broccoli and tomatoes together.

SPICY ROAST BEEF WITH BUTTERNUT SQUASH & CABBAGE

A spicy marinade really brings pizzazz to this roast beef. Ideally, this should be served on the rare side for optimal flavour and texture. The butternut squash and cabbage really soak up the flavours in this one too.

850-g/1 lb. 14 oz. beef roasting joint
300 g/10½ oz. butternut squash, peeled, deseeded and cut into 2-cm/¾-in. pieces
200 g/7 oz. pointed cabbage, sliced

for the marinade
2 teaspoons sea salt
1 teaspoon coconut sugar
1 teaspoon smoked paprika
1 teaspoon garlic powder
1 teaspoon mustard powder
¾ teaspoon dried marjoram or oregano
¼ teaspoon freshly ground black pepper
2 tablespoons olive oil

SERVES 6

First combine the marinade ingredients in a small bowl or ramekin.

Place the beef on a sheet pan with sides large enough to fit the beef and the vegetables in. Rub the marinade all over the beef then cover with foil and leave to marinate for 1 hour at room temperature.

Preheat the oven to 200°C (400°F) Gas 6.

When the hour is up, add the butternut squash to the pan and roast both the beef and the squash together in the preheated oven for 1 hour 10 minutes, still covered in the foil to start with.

Add the cabbage with 30 minutes cooking time left to go and remove the foil. Give everything a good stir at the same time.

When the cooking is done, turn the oven off and take the beef joint out of the oven, then leave it to rest covered in foil, whilst the vegetables rest in the residual heat of the oven.

Once the beef has rested for 10 minutes, slice it thinly and serve with the vegetables.

Serving Suggestion: Serve with Creamy Coleslaw (page 122) and Aubergine Purée (page 125).

BEEF-STUFFED TOMATOES

Actually, it was my father who asked for me to recreate these 'tomate farcie' as we first knew them. A summer holiday back in 1989 to the Alps, where this dish was so in season and we ate far too many of them, was his inspiration. Fast forward nearly 30 years and he suddenly took a fancy for them when he knew I was writing this book.

8 large tomatoes (not beef tomatoes)
250 g/9 oz. minced/ground beef
25 g/¹/₂ cup dried breadcrumbs or finely
    ground cornflakes
25 g/¹/₄ cup ground almonds
¹/₂ onion, roughly chopped
2 tablespoons freshly chopped
    flat leaf parsley
1 tablespoon freshly chopped thyme leaves
40 g/¹/₃ cup Gruyère cheese, grated
¹/₂ teaspoon sea salt
1 tablespoon olive oil
sea salt and freshly ground black pepper

SERVES 4

Preheat the oven to 200°C (400°F) Gas 6.

Cut the tops off the tomatoes, but reserve the tops.

Remove the seeds and flesh of the tomatoes using a serrated edged spoon or a combination of knife and spoon, being careful not to slice the tomatoes.

In a large bowl, mix together the minced/ground beef, breadcrumbs or cornflakes, ground almonds, onion, herbs, grated cheese and ¹/₂ teaspoon salt. Mix this really well, ideally by using your hands.

Put the empty tomatoes on a sheet pan with sides. Stuff each one with some of the beef mixture.

Put the tomato lids back onto the tomatoes, drizzle with olive oil and sprinkle with salt and pepper. Bake in the preheated oven for 30 minutes until the tomatoes are soft and the beef mixture inside is cooked through. Serve.

Serving Suggestion: Serve with Twice Baked Cheesy Potatoes (page 117) and Citrus Fennel Salad (page 122).

STEAK & CHIPS

2 minute steaks
2 sweet potatoes, peeled and cut into
    1-cm/¹/₂-in. chips/fries
1 teaspoon extra virgin olive oil
¹/₂ teaspoon sea salt
10 cherry tomatoes, halved

for the marinade
2 teaspoons balsamic glaze
2 tablespoons olive oil
¹/₄ teaspoon Dijon mustard
¹/₄ teaspoon garlic salt
¹/₄ teaspoon sea salt

SERVES 2

The key to a quick steak, especially a lower cost minute steak, is the marinade and the length of time the marinade is left on in advance of cooking. This steak dish needs a little advanced planning but not a lot, and is quick and simple as well as being a low cost and healthier way to enjoy steak and 'chips'/'fries'.

For the marinade, mix all of the ingredients together in a bowl or shake in a bottle to combine. Put the steaks in a flat bowl, cover with the marinade and leave to marinate in the refrigerator for 8–12 hours, uncovered, turning a couple of times.

When you're ready to cook, remove the steaks from the refrigerator. Preheat the oven to 200°C (400°F) Gas 6.

Toss the sweet potato chips/fries on a sheet pan with the olive oil and salt. Bake in the preheated oven or 15–20 minutes until cooked. Remove from the pan.

Add the steaks and cherry tomato halves to the sheet pan. Preheat the grill/broiler to high. Grill/broil the steaks for 2 minutes on one side and 1 minute on the other side. Serve the steaks with the sweet potato chips/fries and tomatoes.

SMOKY LAMB RIBS WITH SLOW-ROASTED CARROTS

1 teaspoon coconut sugar
1/2 teaspoon smoked paprika
1/2 teaspoon mustard powder
1/2 teaspoon garlic powder
1/2 teaspoon onion powder
1/4 teaspoon chilli/chili powder
1/4 teaspoon sea salt
1 teaspoon dried oregano
1 teaspoon apple cider vinegar
2 tablespoons olive oil
4 large carrots, cut into 5-cm/2-in. batons
600 g/1 lb. 5 oz. lamb ribs

SERVES 2-3

Such a cost-effective cut of meat and so underrated. Discover how crowd-pleasing flavoursome lamb ribs can be with this recipe and keep your weekly food bill within budget at the same time.

Preheat the oven to 140°C (275°F) Gas 1.

In a small bowl, mix together the sugar, paprika, mustard powder, garlic powder, onion powder, chilli/chili powder, salt, oregano, vinegar and olive oil.

Put the carrot batons on a sheet pan with sides and put the lamb ribs on top of the carrots. Rub the spice mix all over the ribs.

Bake in the preheated oven for 1 hour, then reduce the temperature to 120°C (250°F) Gas 1/2 and cover tightly with foil. Bake for a further 1 1/2 hours. Serve.

Serving Suggestion: Serve with Perfect Roast Potatoes (page 117), or if you want something to cut through the richness of the ribs, try a Citrus Fennel Salad (page 122).

MINTY LAMB BURGERS & VEG

500 g/1 lb. 2 oz. minced/ground lamb
2 shallots, finely diced
1 garlic clove, crushed
10 g/1/3 cup freshly chopped mint
1/2 teaspoon ground cumin
1 teaspoon sea salt
2 medium sweet potatoes, peeled and cut into 3 x 1-cm/1 1/4 x 1/2-in. chips/fries
1/2 cauliflower, chopped into florets
1 teaspoon olive oil

SERVES 4

Mint and lamb make an ideal partnership, and one that continues to work in these moist burgers. It's a very satisfying spring dish.

Preheat the oven to 200°C (400°F) Gas 6.

In a large bowl, mix together the minced/ground lamb, shallots, garlic, mint, cumin and 1/2 teaspoon of the salt thoroughly. Using your hands, form into four large, flat lamb burgers.

Place the sweet potato chips/fries and cauliflower florets on a sheet pan with sides. Drizzle over the olive oil and sprinkle over the remaining salt.

Bake in the preheated oven for 20 minutes. Then add the burgers to the pan and bake for a further 15 minutes. Check the burgers are cooked through. Serve immediately.

Serving Suggestion: Serve with Avocado Mayonnaise and Aubergine Purée (page 125).

LAMB SKEWERS WITH ROASTED VEG

Lamb provides great flavour and works wonderfully well in baked recipes especially, as in this dish, with the complementary flavours of honey, garlic, tomato and tamari.

2 garlic cloves, thinly sliced
2 tablespoons tamari
2 tablespoons tomato purée/paste
1 tablespoon honey
5 sprigs of fresh thyme
800 g/1¾ lb. lamb steak, cut into 2-cm/¾-in. cubes
3 large carrots, sliced thickly on the diagonal about 2-cm/¾-in. thick

2 tablespoons olive oil
2 medium red onions, quartered
2 medium courgettes/zucchini, sliced lengthways, then cut into semi-circles, about 2-cm/¾-in. thick
200 g/7 oz. button mushrooms
sea salt

4 metal skewers

SERVES 4

Preheat the oven to 200°C (400°F) Gas 6.

To make the marinade, mix together the garlic, tamari, tomato purée/paste, honey and the leaves from 2 sprigs of thyme.

Mix the meat with the marinade and leave to marinate whilst preparing and cooking the vegetables.

Put the carrots onto a sheet pan with sides, drizzle over some of the olive oil and add a good pinch of salt and place in the preheated oven. After 10 minutes, add the onions, courgettes/zucchini, mushrooms and the remaining thyme to the pan. Drizzle with the remaining olive oil and a little more salt and bake for a further 15 minutes.

Meanwhile, thread the meat onto four metal skewers. Add these to the sheet pan containing the vegetables. Bake for a further 10 minutes until the meat is just cooked but still tender and all the veg are cooked and ready to eat. Serve.

LAMB KOFTA MEATBALLS & FRAGRANT SWEET POTATO WEDGES

These kofta meatballs are a family favourite of ours. We love them in different forms, whether they're cooked at a family BBQ, a meatball stew, or, as here, simply baked meatballs.

for the meatballs
800 g/1¾ lb. minced/ground lamb
¼ teaspoon ground turmeric
½ teaspoon ground cumin
1 teaspoon garlic granules
1 teaspoon onion powder
1 teaspoon sea salt
1 red onion, finely chopped
2 large garlic cloves, minced
20 g/⅓ cup freshly chopped coriander/cilantro
1 tablespoon honey

for the wedges
1 kg/2¼ lb. sweet potatoes, cut into wedges
1 teaspoon ground cumin
1 teaspoon black onion seeds
½ teaspoon sea salt
1 teaspoon olive oil, ghee or melted coconut oil

SERVES 4

Preheat the oven to 200°C (400°F) Gas 6.

For the wedges, put the sweet potato wedges in a bowl and add the cumin, black onion seeds, salt and olive oil, ghee or coconut oil and mix together. Put the wedges onto a non-stick sheet pan with sides, well-spaced apart, and bake in the preheated oven for 25 minutes, tossing once during cooking.

Meanwhile, make the meatballs. In a large bowl, mix together all the meatball ingredients by hand. Roll into small balls (about 20–25 in total) and, after 25 minutes cooking, place on the same sheet pan as the sweet potato wedges.

Bake in the oven for a further 15 minutes until cooked through. Serve the meatballs with the wedges.

Serving Suggestion: Serve with Avocado Mayonnaise (page 122) and Quinoa Tabbouleh (page 118).

MARINATED LAMB CHOPS WITH GARLICKY TOMATOES & WHITE BEANS

This is a summery dish that requires a little marinating time but is worth the wait. Using relatively few ingredients, you can create a really delicious meal.

8 lamb chops
7 plum tomatoes
3 garlic cloves, peeled
1 x 400-g/14-oz. can cannellini
    or white kidney beans
    (drained and rinsed)
2 tablespoons freshly chopped
    basil
1 teaspoon olive oil
½ teaspoon sea salt
freshly ground black pepper

for the marinade
75 ml/scant ⅓ cup olive oil
40 ml/3 tablespoons red wine
    vinegar
1 teaspoon sea salt

SERVES 4

In a shallow bowl (large enough for all the lamb chops), whisk the marinade ingredients together. Put the lamb chops in the bowl, turn to coat, then cover with foil and marinate in the refrigerator for 2 hours. Remove from the refrigerator 30 minutes before cooking.

Preheat the oven to 200°C (400°F) Gas 6.

Cut the tomatoes in half and lay in a sheet pan with sides with the garlic. Add the marinated lamb and 1 tablespoon of the marinade. Bake in the preheated oven for 15–20 minutes, uncovered, then stir in the beans, basil, olive oil, salt and pepper and crush the softened garlic cloves with the back of a fork as you stir, then taste to check the seasonings.

Put the sheet pan back into the oven with the heat turned off to allow the residual heat to heat the beans. Serve after 5 minutes.

PERFECT ROAST LAMB CHOPS WITH ROSEMARY VEGETABLES

A light but aromatic lamb dish to be enjoyed all year round. These chops are delicious served alongside Cumin Roasted Chickpeas (page 121) and Aubergine Purée (page 125).

8 lamb chops
1½ teaspoons sea salt
500 g/1 lb 2 oz. small new
    potatoes
2 sprigs of fresh rosemary,
    chopped in half
1 tablespoon olive oil

2 garlic cloves, peeled
400 g/14 oz. cherry tomatoes
250 g/9 oz. portabella
    mushrooms, thinly sliced
1 tablespoon balsamic glaze

SERVES 4

Preheat the oven to 220°C (425°F) Gas 7.

Put the lamb chops in a shallow bowl and sprinkle over 1 teaspoon of the salt. Set aside.

Place the potatoes and rosemary in a large sheet pan with sides. Sprinkle the remaining salt over the potatoes, then drizzle over the olive oil. Bake in the preheated oven for 20 minutes.

Add the lamb chops and garlic cloves to the pan and bake for a further 20 minutes. With 10 minutes baking time to go, add the tomatoes and mushrooms to the pan with the balsamic glaze and give everything a stir. Serve when cooked.

7-HOUR LAMB WITH ROASTED CARROTS & CELERIAC

This succulent lamb dish requires very little preparation, but it does take a while to cook. The wait, however, is truly worth it. The earthy sweetness of the slow roasted carrots and celeriac complement the lamb perfectly. If you're missing some greens, you could stir some spinach into the juices once reduced and allow it to wilt before serving.

1 tablespoon sea salt
1 whole leg of lamb (bone in), roughly
    2 kg/4½ lb.
1 tablespoon olive oil
4 large carrots, sliced into
    2–3-cm/³/₄–1¹/₄-in. thick rounds
1 celeriac, peeled and diced
300 ml/1¹/₄ cups dry white wine
300 ml/1¹/₄ cups stock (meat or vegetable)

SERVES 8

Preheat the oven to 120°C (250°F) Gas ½.

Sprinkle the salt evenly over the lamb. Place a sheet pan with high sides on the hob and heat the olive oil. Add the lamb to the sheet pan and sear on all sides until it reaches a lovely brown colour all over. Pour off the excess fat. Add the vegetables to the sheet pan, ensuring everything fits snugly.

Pour the wine and stock into the sheet pan. Put the sheet pan back on the hob and bring to the boil over a medium heat.

Using oven gloves, cover the sheet pan tightly with foil, then place into the preheated oven for 7 hours until cooked, basting twice during the cooking time.

Remove the lamb and vegetables from the sheet pan, place on a warmed plate and cover in foil. Heat the juices on the hob again to reduce.

Carve the lamb and serve with the cooked vegetables and a little of the reduced juices over the top.

HONEY MUSTARD LAMB & PARSNIPS

A delightful mix of honey and mustard that serves to keep this lamb moist and flavoursome. A quick-win as far as roasts go too. One to impress. Serve with Twice Baked Cheesy Potatoes (page 117) for a substantial winter warmer or with Butterbean Purée (page 121) for something a little lighter.

$^1/_2$ leg of lamb, roughly 1 kg/2$^1/_4$ lb.
60 ml/$^1/_4$ cup tamari
2 tablespoons honey
1$^1/_2$ tablespoons wholegrain mustard
2 tablespoons warm water
5 parsnips, peeled and sliced lengthways
   into thirds
4 sprigs of fresh rosemary

SERVES 4

Take the lamb out of the refrigerator an hour before you are ready to cook it.

To make the marinade, mix the tamari, honey, mustard and warm water together in a bowl.

Put the lamb on a sheet pan with high sides and pour the marinade over the top. Leave to marinate for 1 hour, turning over a couple of times whilst marinating.

Preheat the oven to 200°C (400°F) Gas 6.

Put the parsnips and rosemary in the sheet pan with the lamb and tuck under the lamb. Spoon a little of the marinade over the lamb.

Put the sheet pan in the preheated oven and roast the lamb for about 55 minutes for rare adding another 10 minutes for medium.

Remove the lamb from the oven and leave to rest, covered in foil, for 10 minutes, before serving with the parsnips. The parsnips can remain in the oven in the residual heat whilst the lamb rests.

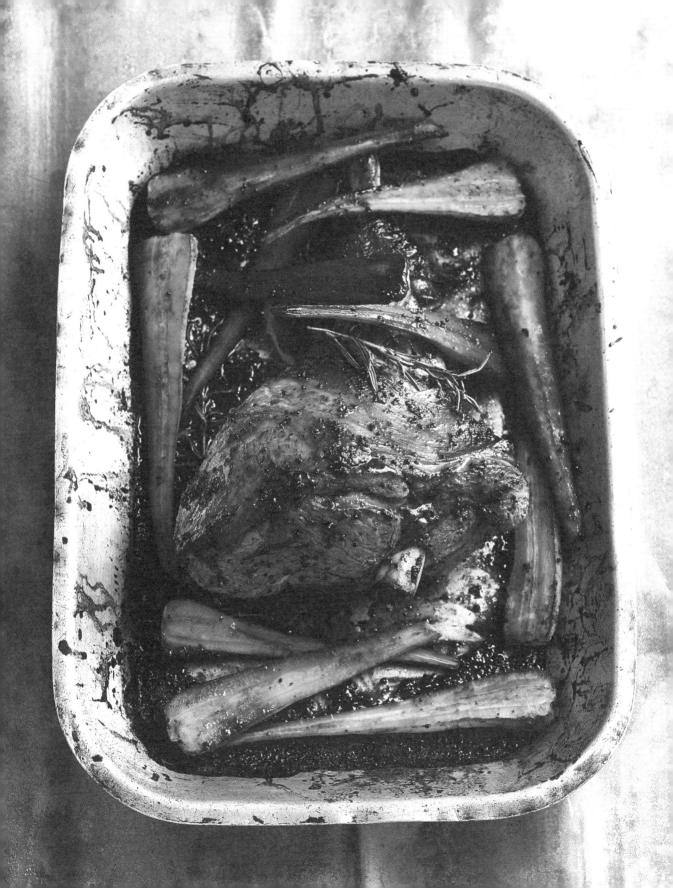

POULTRY

COQ AU VIN

This is a lighter version of the more wintry classic dish made with red wine. This dish is made using white wine, keeping it more summery. A family favourite!

250 g/9 oz. diced unsmoked streaky bacon
6 banana shallots, halved
3 garlic cloves, crushed
1 tablespoon freshly chopped thyme leaves
3 sprigs of fresh rosemary
8 chicken thighs (skin on),
   cut in two if large
3 tablespoons olive oil
250 ml/1 cup plus 1 tablespoon
   dry white wine
350 g/12 oz. mushrooms, cut into quarters
1 x 400-g/14-oz. can white beans, such as
   cannellini, drained and rinsed
sea salt
2 tablespoons freshly chopped
   flat leaf parsley, to serve

SERVES 4

Preheat the oven to 200°C (400°F) Gas 6.

Toss the bacon, shallots, garlic, thyme and rosemary into a sheet pan with sides. Arrange the chicken thighs on top.

Season with salt and drizzle over the olive oil.

Roast in the preheated oven for 20 minutes. Add the wine, mushrooms and white beans and give everything a stir, then roast for another 25 minutes until the chicken is cooked through. Serve, sprinkled with the parsley.

SPANISH RED PEPPER & CHICKEN BAKE

8–10 new potatoes, cut into quarters,
   lengthways
1 teaspoon olive oil
1 teaspoon sea salt
1 onion, finely chopped
1 garlic clove, finely chopped
1 red (bell) pepper, deseeded and
   very finely chopped
1/2 teaspoon marjoram or oregano
3/4 teaspoon smoked paprika
 1 x 400-g/14-oz. can chopped tomatoes
200 g/7 oz. mini chicken fillets
1 tablespoon freshly chopped oregano

SERVES 2

This is a dish that tastes of Spanish holidays. It cooks whilst you plan your next summer vacation.

Preheat the oven to 200°C (400°F) Gas 6.

Put the potatoes on a small sheet pan with sides, drizzle over the olive oil and sprinkle over 1/4 teaspoon salt.

Bake in the preheated oven for 20 minutes. Make sure the potatoes are almost cooked. If not, give them a little longer.

Meanwhile, make the sauce. Combine the onion, garlic, red (bell) pepper, herbs, paprika, the remaining salt and tomatoes in a bowl. Add the chicken and the sauce to the potatoes, then cover with foil and cook in the oven for a further 20 minutes until the chicken is cooked. Sprinkle over the freshly chopped oregano, if desired, and serve.

HARISSA CHICKEN & CHICKPEA BAKE

Succulent spicy chicken and soft melt-in-the-mouth chickpeas, this is a protein-rich meal that feels rather more luxurious than the ingredients would tell us otherwise.

500 g/1 lb. 2 oz. skinless, boneless chicken
   breasts, cut into 4-cm/1 1/2-in. pieces
1 courgette/zucchini, sliced into
   5 mm/1/4-in. rounds
1 onion, cut into 16 slices
2 large, flat mushrooms, thickly sliced
1 teaspoon olive oil
1/2 teaspoon sea salt
1 x 400-g/14-oz. can chickpeas,
   drained and rinsed

for the marinade
1 tablespoon honey or maple syrup
1 1/2 teaspoons harissa spice mix
2 tablespoons olive oil
1/2 teaspoon sea salt

SERVES 4

Preheat the oven to 220°C (425°F) Gas 7.

First make the marinade. Mix the marinade ingredients together in a large bowl. Put the chopped chicken in the bowl with the marinade and stir to coat. Set aside.

Place the courgette/zucchini, onion and mushrooms on a sheet pan with sides, drizzle over the olive oil and sprinkle over the salt. Bake in the preheated oven for 20 minutes, stirring once during baking.

Add the marinated chicken and the marinade to the sheet pan and give everything a good stir. Bake for about 15 minutes more until the chicken is cooked. Check the chicken to see if it is cooked. If not, leave it in the oven for a little longer.

Finally, stir in the chickpeas and place back in the oven for a couple of minutes to warm through. Serve immediately.

Serving Suggestion: Serve with a Simple Salad (page 125) and/or the Aubergine Purée (page 125).

CORNFLAKE CHICKEN NUGGETS WITH SWEET POTATO CHIPS & ROASTED CHERRY TOMATOES

One of my children has a friend who really prefers classic children's foods to a range of adult flavours so when she comes round I tend to modify our recipes a little. These nuggets were, according to her, 'the best nuggets I have ever tasted'. I am taking that as a compliment!

2 medium sweet potatoes,
    peeled and sliced into 1-cm/¹/₂-in. thick
    chips/fries
1 teaspoon olive oil
³/₄ teaspoon sea salt
120 g/5 cups cornflakes
1 egg
125 ml/¹/₂ cup dairy or non-dairy milk
1 tablespoon arrowroot powder
¹/₄ teaspoon garlic salt
4 skinless, boneless chicken breasts, chopped
    into 4 x 2-cm/1¹/₂ x ³/₄-in. nuggets
16 cherry tomatoes on the vine

SERVES 4

Preheat the oven to 200°C (400°F) Gas 6.

Put the sweet potatoes on a sheet pan with sides, drizzle over the olive oil and sprinkle over ¹/₂ teaspoon salt. Bake in the preheated oven for 35 minutes.

Meanwhile, grind the cornflakes in a food processor to fine crumbs. Alternatively, put the cornflakes in a freezer bag, close the bag tightly and bash the cornflakes with a rolling pin. Place in a bowl.

In another small bowl, whisk the egg, add the milk, arrowroot, garlic salt and ¹/₄ teaspoon salt.

Dip the chicken nuggets into the egg mixture, then into the cornflakes to cover and put onto a separate sheet pan. Put the chicken nuggets in the oven with the potatoes for the last 10 minutes of baking. Add the tomatoes to the sweet potato sheet pan for the last 10 minutes. Serve immediately.

CHICKEN NUGGETS WITH ROASTED TOMATOES, OLIVES & ASPARAGUS

This is a fantastically simple gluten-free chicken nugget recipe that's quick to make and complemented by moist and succulent baked tomatoes, olives and asparagus.

600 g/3¹/₂ cups cherry tomatoes, halved
20 asparagus tips
6 garlic cloves, halved
1 tablespoon olive oil
¹/₂ teaspoon sea salt
2 x 85-g/3-oz. bags plantain chips
2 teaspoons garlic powder
1 x 190-g/7-oz. jar red pesto
4 skinless, boneless chicken breasts,
    sliced into mini fillets
1 x 190-g/7-oz. jar pitted black olives,
    drained (110-g/4-oz. drained weight)

SERVES 4

Preheat the oven to 200°C (400°F) Gas 6.

Spread the tomatoes and asparagus out on a sheet pan with sides and scatter over the garlic cloves. Drizzle over the olive oil and sprinkle over the salt. Roast in the preheated oven for 15 minutes.

To make the chicken nuggets, crush the plantain chips into a breadcrumb consistency in a food processor or in a plastic bag with a rolling pin. Put the plantain crumbs into a bowl and stir in the garlic powder. Put the red pesto in a separate bowl. Dip each mini chicken fillet into the red pesto, then into the crushed plantain/garlic powder mix to coat.

When the tomatoes and asparagus have been baking for 15 minutes, add the olives to the pan, and place the chicken nuggets on a separate sheet pan and bake for a further 12 minutes. Check the nuggets are cooked through. Serve.

CHEAT'S CHICKEN KIEV WITH TOMATOES, COURGETTES & ROASTED NEW POTATOES

20 medium new potatoes,
  diced into 15-mm/⅝-in. cubes
1 tablespoon olive oil
4 skinless, boneless chicken breasts
2 garlic cloves, peeled
10 g/½ cup fresh flat leaf parsley,
  including stalks
60 g/4 tablespoons salted butter, softened
12 cherry tomatoes
1 courgette/zucchini, cut into
  1-cm/½-in. thick slices
½ teaspoon garlic salt

SERVES 4

Kids will love this! It's a lot like the processed version in taste except this version is real. Believe me when I say that they'll not miss the breadcrumbs.

Preheat the oven to 200°C (400°F) Gas 6.

Place the new potatoes on a sheet pan, add the olive oil and mix to coat.

Create four foil or baking parchment rectangles (with enough excess to fold over the chicken) and place a chicken breast on each.

Using a sharp knife, slice down the length of the top of the chicken breasts, but don't cut right through.

In a food processor, finely chop the garlic and parsley and then mix in the butter. Divide the mixture between the chicken breast pockets.

Add three cherry tomatoes and some courgette/zucchini slices to each parcel and sprinkle over the garlic salt. Close the parcels up, then nestle them in amongst the potatoes, clearing potatoes out from under each parcel on the sheet pan. Bake in the preheated oven for 30–35 minutes until the potatoes and chicken breasts are cooked through.

Serving Suggestion: Serve with baked sweet potatoes.

ROASTED CHICKEN THIGHS WITH PLUMS & TARRAGON

There's an invasion of Scandinavian influence in the UK right now and I, for one, welcome it, especially when it means cheap quality furniture and some unusual but delicious culinary influences too. This combination of chicken, plums and tarragon is inspired by a Scandinavian original.

8 chicken thighs
2 teaspoons garlic salt
20 g/1 cup fresh tarragon
4 large plums, halved and
  stoned/pitted
5 shallots, halved

1 head of broccoli,
  cut into florets
2 teaspoons olive oil
freshly ground black pepper

SERVES 4

Preheat the oven to 190°C (375°F) Gas 5.

Put the chicken pieces on a sheet pan with deep sides.

Add the garlic salt, tarragon, plums, shallots and pepper, to taste.

Bake in the preheated oven for 45–50 minutes until the chicken is cooked through.

With 20 minutes to go, add the broccoli to the pan, drizzle over the olive oil and continue to bake. Serve.

CHICKEN FAJITAS WITH MILD GUACAMOLE

This is a very popular and sociable meal. Simply lay all of the elements out on the table and let people help themselves. Try stopping my two children from going back for seconds and thirds of this dish!

800 g/1¾ lb. boneless, skinless chicken breasts, cut into strips
2 orange (bell) peppers, deseeded and sliced
2 courgettes/zucchini, sliced
2 onions, halved and sliced
1 x 28-g/1-oz. pack fajita seasoning (try and avoid the ones that have sugar as their prime ingredient)
4 tablespoons olive oil
8 tortilla wraps or lettuce leaves

for the guacamole
2 ripe avocados, peeled and stoned/pitted
5 g/¼ cup fresh coriander/cilantro, stems and leaves
70 g/2½ oz. red onion, finely diced
½ tablespoon freshly squeezed lime juice
1 plum tomato, peeled and deseeded
40 g/4 tablespoons extra virgin olive oil
sea salt and freshly ground black pepper, to taste
lime wedges, to serve

SERVES 4

Preheat the oven to 220°C (425°F) Gas 7.

In a large bowl, mix together the chicken strips, (bell) peppers, courgettes/zucchini and onions. In a separate bowl, mix the fajita seasoning and olive oil, then combine the seasoning/oil mix with the chicken mix and stir to make sure everything is coated evenly.

Spread this mix out on a large sheet pan.

Bake in the preheated oven for 15 minutes or until the chicken is cooked through and the vegetables are soft, stirring once.

Meanwhile, make the guacamole. Put all the guacamole ingredients into a food processor and blend.

Finally, just before you remove the chicken and vegetables from the oven, warm the tortillas or prepare the lettuce leaves. Serve the fajita chicken and vegetables with the guacamole and the wraps/lettuce leaves. Serve with lime wedges for squeezing over.

MOROCCAN CHICKEN

The root vegetables and apples in this recipe serve not only to soak up the delicious cooking juices from the chicken but also to provide a contrast in texture and flavour to the gentle Moroccan spices.

1 large oven-ready chicken (approx.
  1.7 kg/3³/₄ lb.)
2¹/₂ teaspoons sea salt
500 g/1 lb. 2 oz. carrots, quartered lengthways
500 g/1 lb. 2 oz. sweet potatoes, peeled and
  cut into 15 mm/⁵/₈-in. discs
3 Granny Smith apples, quartered and cored
zest and juice of 1 large orange
250 ml/generous 1 cup chicken stock
250 ml/generous 1 cup dry white wine
1 tablespoon grated (peeled) fresh ginger
2 teaspoons ras-el-hanout or a Moroccan
  spice mix

SERVES 4

Preheat the oven to 200°C (400°F) Gas 6.

Find a roasting pan large enough for the chicken, vegetables, fruit and liquid to fit in.

Put the chicken in the roasting pan. Season the skin of the chicken with the salt. Arrange the carrots, sweet potatoes and apples around the chicken.

Mix the orange zest and juice, stock, wine, ginger and ras-el-hanout together in a bowl and pour over the chicken and vegetables.

Bake in the preheated oven for 1 hour 25 minutes, basting frequently. Cover the chicken with foil after half the cooking time to ensure the outside is not overcooked. Serve.

ROAST CHICKEN & BEANS WITH ROOT VEGETABLES

This dish is what my husband describes as 'a proper feed'. It's a tasty, filling all-in-one dish, combining winter vegetables and white beans with succulent roasted chicken. A dish that can be made for any occasion.

3 tablespoons olive oil
1 large oven-ready chicken (approx.
  1.7 kg/3³/₄ lb.)
1 lemon, halved
2 large leeks, thickly sliced
¹/₂ swede/rutabaga, peeled and diced into
  1-cm/¹/₂-in. cubes
6 baby parsnips or 2 large parsnips,
  peeled and sliced into
  6 x 2 cm/2¹/₂ x ³/₄-in. fingers
500 g/1 lb. 2 oz. Brussels sprouts
  (untrimmed weight), trimmed and halved
4 large garlic cloves, halved
1 tablespoon plus 1 teaspoon balsamic glaze
2 tablespoons freshly chopped thyme leaves
1 x 400-g/14-oz. can white beans, drained
  and rinsed
sea salt and freshly ground black pepper

SERVES 6

Preheat the oven to 200°C (400°F) Gas 6.

Heat 1 tablespoon of the olive oil in a very large sheet pan with sides (a large joint roasting pan should work here) in the preheated oven for 3 minutes. Add the whole chicken, placing it skin-side down initially, then immediately turn it over and rest breast-side up on the sheet pan. Season generously with salt and pepper and place the lemon halves inside the cavity of the chicken.

Put the chicken in the preheated oven and roast for 1 hour 25 minutes.

Put all of the prepared vegetables and garlic into a large bowl and stir in another 1 tablespoon of the olive oil and 1 tablespoon of the balsamic glaze with a pinch of salt, a twist of pepper and the chopped thyme.

50 minutes before the end of the chicken's roasting time, add the vegetables to the sheet pan and baste the chicken with the juices. Stir twice and baste the chicken twice more whilst they both cook. Take the chicken out of the sheet pan, stir in the beans and the remaining balsamic glaze and let them sit in the oven with the door shut and the oven turned off to heat through. Carve the chicken, then remove the vegetable/beans from the oven and serve.

GARLIC ROASTED CHICKEN WITH SHALLOTS & CARROTS

Soft and succulent roasted chicken and sweet roasted shallots and carrots, is a winning combination for a celebration meal.

500 g/1 lb. 2 oz. carrots, sliced in half
400 g/14 oz. shallots, halved lengthways
1 large garlic bulb, sliced in half horizontally
1.5 kg/3¼ lb. whole chicken
70 g/5 tablespoons butter or ghee
   (at room temperature)
1½ tablespoons dry white wine
200 ml/generous ¾ cup fresh chicken stock
150 g/5½ oz. baby spinach
sea salt and freshly ground black pepper

SERVES 4-6

Preheat the oven to 200°C (400°F) Gas 6.

Put the carrots, shallots, garlic and chicken into a roasting pan. Smother the chicken with the butter or ghee and season well with salt and pepper.

Roast in the preheated oven for 45 minutes, basting twice.

Meanwhile, place the wine and stock in a large saucepan and stir. After 45 minutes, add the vegetables from the chicken pan to this pan and remove the garlic. Squeeze the soft garlic pulp out into the vegetable/stock mixture and discard the skin.

Cover the chicken with foil and roast for a further 30 minutes, basting once.

Heat the saucepan with the wine, stock and vegetables in and simmer gently for the remainder of the chicken roasting time. Add the spinach and stir until wilted. Remove from the heat.

Check that the chicken is cooked through, then leave it to rest. Carve and serve the chicken with some of the cooked veg and a little of the stock over the top.

Serving Suggestion: Serve with Perfect Roasted Potatoes (page 117).

DUCK IN ORANGE GLAZE ON A BED OF LEEKS AND MUSHROOMS

This dish is a modern take on the heavy and sugary duck a l'orange of the 1980s. The duck combines with melt-in-the-mouth leeks and mushrooms. A fine dish!

freshly squeezed juice of ½ orange
3 heaped tablespoons St. Dalfour Thick Cut Orange Spread/bitter Seville orange marmalade
1 teaspoon red wine vinegar
2 boneless duck breasts, each about 170 g/ 6 oz., skin on
2 large leeks, cut in half lengthways and into 1-cm/½-in. slices
200 g/7 oz. chestnut mushrooms, halved
sea salt and freshly ground black pepper

SERVES 2

Preheat the oven to 190°C (375°F) Gas 5.

In a small bowl, mix together the orange juice, orange spread and vinegar, plus some salt and pepper, to create a glaze.

Lay the duck breasts skin-side up in a sheet pan and spread the glaze over the top. Leave to marinate whilst you prepare your vegetables.

Put the vegetables in the sheet pan alongside the duck and give the vegetables a good stir. Season with salt and pepper.

Bake in the preheated oven for 30 minutes, but baste the duck breasts once and stir the vegetables well to make sure they are cooking evenly. Serve.

DUCK LEGS WITH APPLE, PARSNIP & WHITE CABBAGE

This is a substantial winter dish. When you need comfort, look straight over at this recipe. Sweet and succulent duck combines with moist and flavoursome cabbage that has been allowed to soak up an abundance of flavour from the rest of the dish.

4 duck legs
1 tablespoon sea salt
5 large parsnips, peeled and halved
1 white cabbage, cored and cut into 10 portions
4 Granny Smith apples, halved and cored
½ teaspoon ground cloves
½ teaspoon ground allspice

SERVES 4

Preheat the oven to 180°C (350°F) Gas 4.

Place the duck legs in a large roasting pan and season well with the salt.

Bake in the preheated oven for 20 minutes, then baste with the juices released from the legs and add the vegetables and apples, turning those over in the juices too. Sprinkle the spices over the dish.

Bake for another 1 hour 20 minutes, turning the vegetables and legs three times whilst cooking. Serve.

Serving Suggestion: Serve with a green salad.

FISH

THAI SALMON BAKE

Whilst salmon is one of our prime sources of omega-3 fatty acids, it is not always everyone's favourite. Baking it in this light Thai sauce adds flavour but also helps to keep the salmon really moist. It should simply fall apart when a fork is pushed into it. You can make this spicier if palates in your household prefer.

2 garlic cloves, crushed
2-cm/³/₄-in. piece of ginger, peeled and finely chopped
1 x 400-g/14-oz. can coconut milk
1 tablespoon unrefined or coconut sugar
1¹/₂ teaspoons Thai 7 Spice seasoning
2 tablespoons fish sauce
1 tablespoon freshly squeezed lime juice
3 banana shallots, finely chopped
2 tablespoons freshly chopped coriander/ cilantro
4 salmon fillets (approx. 140 g/5 oz.), skin on
250 g/9 oz. asparagus spears, cut into 2-cm/³/₄-in. pieces

SERVES 4

Preheat the oven to 200°C (400°F) Gas 6.

Put the garlic, ginger, coconut milk, sugar, Thai 7 Spice seasoning, fish sauce and lime juice in a medium-sized bowl and mix together. Add the shallots and coriander/cilantro to the mixture. Alternatively, put the garlic, ginger, shallots and coriander into a food processor and chop, then add the coconut milk, fish sauce, sugar, Thai 7 Spice seasoning and lime juice and mix again.

Put the salmon, skin side down, and the asparagus slices on a sheet pan.

Pour the sauce mix over the top of the salmon and asparagus. Cover with foil and bake in the preheated oven for 35 minutes. Serve.

Note if using wild salmon, you may want to add this 15 minutes into the cooking time to keep it moist, as wild salmon naturally contains less fat.

Serving Suggestion: Serve with boiled basmati rice, quinoa or Egg Fried Cauliflower Rice (page 118).

SMOKED SALMON MUFFINS

If you are a fan of salmon and scrambled eggs, then you'll love these muffins. They're light and delicious. A mix of salmon saltiness and smooth creamy egg with a snap of chive. They're great hot or cold.

4 eggs
100 g/3¹/₂ oz. smoked salmon, roughly chopped
2 spring onions/scallions, sliced into 5-mm/¹/₄-in. pieces
1 tablespoon grated Parmesan or Pecorino cheese
¹/₄ teaspoon freshly ground black pepper

muffin pan, lightly greased with olive oil

SERVES 2

Preheat the oven to 200°C (400°F) Gas 6.

Put the eggs, salmon, spring onions/scallions, cheese and black pepper in a bowl and whisk together.

Pour an equal amount of the mixture into four of the muffin pan holes.

Bake in the preheated oven for 15–20 minutes until the muffins are fully cooked with no runny egg present. Serve.

Serving Suggestion: Serve with slices of avocado and fresh tomatoes, with a little chopped fresh basil, olive oil, salt and pepper over the top.

TOMATO PESTO HALIBUT WITH GREEN VEG

Packed full of flavour, this tomato pesto topping really brings the halibut to life. It's quick to create the pesto and simple to make the dish.

250 g/9 oz. asparagus tips
300 g/10½ oz. tenderstem
   broccoli
1 large courgette/zucchini,
   cut into 2-cm/¾-in. pieces
1 tablespoon olive oil
4 halibut fillets, skin on, approx.
   2.5-cm/1-in. thick (each about
   200 g/7 oz.)
sea salt and freshly ground
   black pepper

for the tomato pesto
60 g/4 cups fresh basil leaves
70 g/½ cup walnuts, toasted
110 g/1 cup sun-dried tomatoes
   in oil, drained
1 large garlic clove, peeled
5 tablespoons olive oil

SERVES 4

Preheat the oven to 200°C (400°F) Gas 6.

For the pesto, combine the basil leaves, toasted walnuts, sun-dried tomatoes and garlic in a food processor then add the olive oil and combine again to make a paste.

Put the vegetables on a sheet pan, drizzle over the olive oil and season with salt and pepper. Bake in the preheated oven for 20 minutes.

Meanwhile, create four foil or baking parchment parcels. Put one halibut fillet into each parcel and cover each fillet with a thick layer of the tomato pesto. Close up the parcels and put them on the sheet pan with the vegetables. Bake both the vegetables and fish for a further 12 minutes.

Check the fish is just cooked, then serve immediately.

MEDITERRANEAN BAKED FISH FILLETS

This is a simple summer all-in-one fish dish that you'll enjoy eating in the sun (if you can find some).

8 cherry tomatoes, thinly sliced
6 spring onions/scallions, thinly
   sliced on the diagonal
1 tablespoon freshly chopped
   parsley
1 courgette/zucchini, very thinly
   sliced
freshly squeezed juice of
   ½ lemon

2 tablespoons fish stock
   or dry white wine
1 tablespoon olive oil
1½ teaspoons sea salt
3 white fish fillets

SERVES 3

Preheat the oven to 200°C (400°F) Gas 6.

Put the sliced tomatoes, spring onions/scallions, parsley, courgette/zucchini, lemon juice, stock or white wine, olive oil and salt in a bowl and mix together.

Create three foil or baking parchment parcels. Put one fish fillet in each parcel and top with the tomato mix.

Close up the parcels tightly, put them on a sheet pan and bake in the preheated oven for 20 minutes until cooked.

Remove from the oven and serve with a Simple Salad (page 125).

COD BAKED IN TOMATO & OLIVE SAUCE

The sauce in this fish recipe keeps the dish deliciously moist and seeps into the cod
fillets making them even more succulent. A great dish for reluctant fish eaters!

2 onions, finely chopped
2 garlic cloves, finely chopped
10 g/6 tablespoons freshly chopped parsley
600 g/1 lb. 5 oz. canned chopped tomatoes
1 teaspoon sea salt
4 medium cod fillets
2 courgettes/zucchini, very thinly sliced
100 g/1 cup pitted green olives
2 teaspoons olive oil

SERVES 4

Preheat the oven to 200°C (400°F) Gas 6.

Put the onion, garlic and parsley in a medium-sized bowl, mix together, then
add the chopped tomatoes and salt and stir to combine.

Put the cod fillets on a sheet pan with deep sides. Pour some of the tomato
mixture over the top. Add the courgettes/zucchini and olives to the sheet pan
and cover in the remaining tomato mixture. Drizzle over the olive oil.

Bake in the preheated oven for 10–15 minutes until the cod fillets are just
cooked. Serve.

Serving Suggestion: Serve with a green salad.

COD LOIN WITH BALSAMIC FENNEL

Whilst fennel is a love it or hate it kind of vegetable, with the addition of balsamic glaze and alongside baked
cod, this dish really comes alive. You may even discover that not as many people dislike fennel as claim they do.

2 fennel bulbs, sliced into
    2-cm/³⁄₄-in. wedges
1 tablespoon balsamic glaze
2 tablespoons olive oil
2 teaspoons sea salt
4 thick cod loins
1 x 400-g/14-oz. can cherry tomatoes
1 teaspoon coconut sugar or honey
3 tablespoons freshly chopped parsley
freshly ground black pepper

SERVES 4

Preheat the oven to 220°C (425°F) Gas 7.

Put the fennel wedges on a sheet pan. Drizzle over the balsamic glaze,
1 tablespoon of the olive oil and 1 teaspoon salt. Bake in the preheated
oven for 15 minutes. Toss once during baking.

Meanwhile, lay the fish on a smaller sheet pan with sides so that the fillets
fit snugly.

Pour over the cherry tomatoes, coconut sugar or honey, chopped parsley,
the remaining 1 tablespoon olive oil and 1 teaspoon salt and a pinch of
pepper.

Bake for a further 15–20 minutes until the fish is cooked through and the
fennel is crisp at the edges. Serve.

LEMON & BUTTER BAKED SALMON WITH SPRING VEGETABLES

'Spring' and 'simple' are the words that come to mind with this meal. It's all about simple flavours and even simpler techniques, and it celebrates the flavours of Spring!

8 new potatoes, cut into 1-cm/¹/₂-in. pieces
1¹/₂ teaspoons olive oil
1 teaspoon sea salt
8 asparagus spears, trimmed
10 cherry tomatoes
6 mushrooms, chopped into quarters
2 salmon fillets
40 g/3 tablespoons butter
2 lemon slices
freshly ground black pepper

SERVES 2

Preheat the oven to 200°C (400°F) Gas 6.

Lay the potatoes on a sheet pan. Drizzle over the olive oil and sprinkle over ¹/₂ teaspoon of the salt. Bake in the preheated oven for 10 minutes.

Add the asparagus, tomatoes and mushrooms to the sheet pan and stir. Bake for a further 10 minutes.

Add the salmon fillets with a large knob of butter and a slice of lemon on top of each, and sprinkle over the remaining salt and some black pepper.

Bake for a further 10–12 minutes until the salmon is just cooked. Serve.

WHITE FISH & CHORIZO BAKE

1 red (bell) pepper, deseeded and thinly sliced
1 red onion, thinly sliced
1 courgette/zucchini, cut into 1-cm/¹/₂-in. slices
1¹/₂ teaspoons olive oil
75 g/¹/₂ cup finely chopped chorizo
1 lemon, quartered lengthways
2 vines of cherry tomatoes (about 10 on each)
2 white fish fillets
1 teaspoon smoked paprika
³/₄ teaspoon sea salt
freshly chopped parsley, to garnish

SERVES 2

This is an ideal surf and turf meal. Spicy chorizo combined with mellow white fish, gives this dish a real depth of flavour.

Preheat the oven to 200°C (400°F) Gas 6.

Put the (bell) pepper, onion and courgette/zucchini on a sheet pan and drizzle over the olive oil. Stir the vegetables, then bake in the preheated oven for 20 minutes.

Remove the sheet pan from the oven and add the chorizo and lemon quarters, then the vine tomatoes and fish fillets on top. Sprinkle over the paprika and salt and bake for a further 12 minutes. Remove from the oven and check the fish is just cooked, then serve. If the fish is not cooked, then leave in the oven for up to 4 more minutes to cook through. Sprinkle over the parsley, to garnish.

CAJUN SALMON WITH CRISPY LEEKS & BUTTERNUT SQUASH

Wham, bam, thank you mam! This dish is a flavour-packed way to enjoy omega-3 rich salmon. Only ever so slightly spicy and the Cajun spices contrast well with the mellow leeks and baked squash.

2 leeks, sliced lengthways, then into 15-mm/⁵⁄₈-in. thick semi-circles
½ butternut squash, peeled, deseeded and cut into 1-cm/½-in. cubes
1 tablespoon plus 2 teaspoons olive oil
1³⁄₄ teaspoons sea salt
1 teaspoon smoked paprika
1 teaspoon coconut or unrefined sugar
1 garlic clove, crushed
½ teaspoon onion powder
½ teaspoon mustard powder
½ teaspoon finely grated lemon zest
⅛ teaspoon dried marjoram or oregano
⅛ teaspoon dried thyme
1 teaspoon red wine vinegar
4 salmon fillets (about 125 g/4½ oz. each)
lemon wedges, to serve

SERVES 4

Preheat the oven to 200°C (400°F) Gas 6.

Put the vegetables on a sheet pan with sides with 1 tablespoon olive oil and 1 teaspoon salt and toss to mix.

Bake in the preheated oven for 20 minutes.

Meanwhile, prepare the topping for the salmon. In a bowl, mix together the smoked paprika, ³⁄₄ teaspoon salt, sugar, garlic, onion powder, mustard powder, lemon zest, herbs, red wine vinegar and 2 teaspoons olive oil.

Lay the salmon fillets out on a plate and smother each with an equal amount of the topping.

Add the salmon fillets to the sheet pan with the vegetables, and reduce the oven to 180°C (350°F) Gas 4. Bake for a further 15 minutes until cooked.

Serve the salmon on a bed of leeks and butternut squash with lemon wedges for squeezing.

INDIAN PRAWNS WITH CAULIFLOWER

Indian food is synonymous with both prawns/shrimp and cauliflower. Here the two are combined in a curry. It's mild and one to be lapped up by all family members.

1 cauliflower, chopped into
   florets
2 teaspoons sea salt
1 tablespoon olive oil
1 onion, finely chopped
1$^{1}/_{2}$ tablespoons freshly chopped
   coriander/cilantro
2 garlic cloves, crushed
5 mm/$^{1}/_{4}$ in. finger of fresh
   ginger, peeled and grated
1 teaspoon ground cumin
$^{1}/_{2}$ teaspoon ground turmeric
$^{1}/_{4}$ teaspoon ground coriander
$^{1}/_{8}$ teaspoon ground cinnamon
1 x 400-g/14-oz. can coconut
   milk
1 x 400-g/14-oz. can chopped
   tomatoes
225 g/8 oz. frozen king prawns/
   shrimp
1 tablespoon freshly chopped
   coriander/cilantro (optional)

SERVES 4

Preheat the oven to 200°C (400°F) Gas 6.

Place the cauliflower florets on a sheet pan with sides. Sprinkle over 1 teaspoon of the salt and drizzle over the olive oil. Bake in the preheated oven for 30 minutes.

Meanwhile, make the sauce with the onion, coriander/cilantro, garlic, ginger, spices, coconut milk, chopped tomatoes and the remaining salt. You can do this by mixing these ingredients in a bowl or preferably in a food processor.

Add the sauce and prawns/shrimp to the sheet pan, stir and bake for a further 20 minutes until cooked. Sprinkle over the freshly chopped coriander/cilantro, if using, and serve.

TAMARI AND GINGER SALMON WITH ROASTED NEW POTATOES & ASPARAGUS

There's a little marinating time involved in this recipe if you can spare it. The best results will come from marinating all day. A little preparation in the morning will mean a greater tasting dish that evening. It's worth it too because the salmon will just flake away and each mouthful will provide the winning taste combination of honey, ginger and tamari.

4 salmon fillets
400 g/14 oz. baby new potatoes,
   cut to the same size as the
   smallest whole potato
1 teaspoon olive oil
$^{1}/_{8}$ teaspoon sea salt
150 g/5$^{1}/_{2}$ oz. fine asparagus tips,
   sliced into 2-cm/$^{3}/_{4}$-in. lengths

for the marinade
70 ml/scant $^{1}/_{3}$ cup tamari
1 generous tablespoon honey
2 garlic cloves, crushed
10 g/1 tablespoon freshly grated
   ginger (peeled)

SERVES 4

To make the marinade, combine the tamari, honey, garlic and ginger in a flat bowl. Add the salmon fillets to the bowl, turn to coat and ensure they are all sitting in the marinade. Cover the bowl and place in the refrigerator for 8 hours.

When you are ready to cook, preheat the oven to 200°C (400°F) Gas 6.

Prepare the potatoes and put them on a sheet pan with sides. Drizzle over the olive oil and sprinkle over the salt. Bake in the preheated oven for 20 minutes. Check they are almost soft on the inside, then add the salmon, 2 tablespoons of the marinade and the asparagus to the pan.

Bake for a further 10–15 minutes until the salmon just flakes away when you push it down with a fork. Serve.

ROASTED MONKFISH & PARMA HAM PARCELS ON DILL POTATOES

Monkfish is a really substantial, almost 'meaty' fish, so even some non-fish-lovers will be converted by this dish. What better way to serve it than wrapped in salty Parma ham/prosciutto with summery dill potatoes and courgettes/zucchini?

500 g/1 lb. 2 oz. new potatoes washed and quartered

1 tablespoon olive oil

1 teaspoon sea salt

1 medium courgette/zucchini, sliced lengthways and into 1.5-cm/$\frac{1}{2}$-in. thick semi-circles

1 teaspoon dried dill or 2 teaspoons freshly chopped dill

4 skinless, boneless monkfish portions, approx. 140–150 g/5–5$\frac{1}{2}$ oz. each

8 sun-dried tomato slices, from a jar in oil, drained and thinly sliced

2 teaspoons butter

1 tablespoon freshly squeezed lemon juice

$\frac{1}{4}$ teaspoon cracked black pepper

8 slices of Parma ham/prosciutto

SERVES 4

Preheat the oven to 200°C (400°F) Gas 6.

Place the potatoes on a sheet pan with sides. Drizzle over $\frac{1}{2}$ tablespoon of the olive oil and $\frac{1}{2}$ teaspoon salt. Bake in the preheated oven for 15 minutes.

Add the courgette/zucchini to the pan containing the potatoes. Add the remaining olive oil and salt and the dill and stir. Bake the potatoes and courgettes/zucchini for another 10 minutes.

Meanwhile, prepare the fish. Create a deep incision along the top of each fish portion and tuck some of the sun-dried tomato slices and $\frac{1}{2}$ teaspoon of butter. Squeeze over the lemon juice, sprinkle over the black pepper, then wrap each portion in two slices of Parma ham/prosciutto.

Place the fish parcels onto the sheet pan and bake for another 10 minutes or until the fish is just cooked.

Serve immediately.

VEGETARIAN

BLACK BEAN & SWEETCORN HASH

This hash is all about texture. With each mouthful your mouth explodes with the sweet kernels of corn that contrast with the smooth, soft and satisfying black beans. A rainbow of colours is on show with this dish. It's a nice one to serve in the middle of the table and let people help themselves.

2 medium sweet potatoes, peeled and cut into 1.5-cm/^{1}/$_2$-in. cubes
1 medium courgette/zucchini, cut into 1.5-cm/^{1}/$_2$-in. cubes
1 red (bell) pepper, cut into 1.5-cm/^{5}/$_8$-in. pieces
4 large mushrooms, cut into 1.5-cm/^{1}/$_2$-in. cubes
1 x 400-g/14-oz. can black beans, drained and rinsed
130 g/15 oz. canned sweetcorn
3 tablespoons olive oil
^{3}/$_4$ teaspoon garlic salt
^{1}/$_2$ teaspoon sea salt
1 teaspoon sweet smoked paprika
4 UK large/US extra-large eggs
freshly ground black pepper

SERVES 2
AS A MAIN MEAL

Preheat the oven to 200°C (400°F) Gas 6.

Place the sweet potatoes, courgette/zucchini, (bell) pepper, mushrooms, black beans and sweetcorn onto a sheet pan with sides.

Drizzle over the olive oil, sprinkle over the garlic salt, salt and paprika and give everything a good stir. Bake in the preheated oven for 30 minutes. Stir once during cooking.

Remove from the oven after 30 minutes, make four wells in the vegetables then crack an egg into each well.

Bake for a further 7–9 minutes until the eggs are just cooked but the yolks are still runny. Season with black pepper and serve.

BAKED FRITTATA

An extremely versatile dish that allows some flexibility in adding your own leftover vegetables to the mix, to create a filling egg-based tray bake.

2 large red onions, halved and sliced
10 mushrooms, stalks removed and
   cut into thick slices
1 tablespoon olive oil
8 eggs
2 tablespoons mixed freshly chopped herbs
sea salt and freshly ground black pepper

a 20 x 20-cm/8 x 8-in. sheet pan with sides

SERVES 4

Preheat the oven to 200°C (400°F) Gas 6.

Lay the onion and mushroom slices out on the sheet pan. Drizzle over the olive oil.

Bake in the preheated oven for 15 minutes until soft. Turn the vegetables over with a spoon once during cooking.

Meanwhile, whisk together the eggs, herbs and seasoning in a large bowl.

When the vegetables are soft, pour the egg mixture over the vegetables and bake for a further 15 minutes until the egg mix is cooked. Serve.

Serving Suggestion: Serve the frittata in slices with the Simple Salad with Dressing (page 125).

Variation: When you add the egg mix you can also add leftover vegetables or small tomato halves.

BLACK BEAN NACHOS

A fantastic sharing dish for when you have friends over and you have little time to prepare something. Watch everyone dig in with delight!

1 x 400-g/14-oz. can black beans,
   drained and rinsed
1 x 230-g/8-oz. pot fresh salsa
1/2 teaspoon sea salt
100 g/3 1/2 oz. tortilla chips
120 g/1 packed cup plus 3 tablespoons
   grated Cheddar cheese
Guacamole (page 51), to serve
soured cream, to serve

SERVES 2-4

Preheat the oven to 220°C (425°F) Gas 7.

Combine the black beans, salsa and salt in a food processor to make a thick paste.

Spread the paste in the base of a sheet pan with sides. Top with the tortilla chips and then add the cheese.

Bake in the preheated oven for 10 minutes or until the cheese has melted.

Serve immediately with the guacamole and soured cream.

HARISSA-BAKED AVOCADO, BUTTERNUT SQUASH & EGGS

The addition of spicy harissa to the already colourful flavour and texture combination of green avocado, bright orange butternut squash and eggs, is the ideal way to marry all of these ingredients together. It's rich and tangy in flavour, but the mellowness of the other ingredients contrasts well.

2 tablespoons harissa paste
2 tablespoons olive oil
550 g/1¼ lb. butternut squash, peeled, deseeded and roughly chopped into 2-cm/¾-in. cubes
60 g/½ cup pitted/stoned black olives
15 cherry tomatoes
1 ripe avocado, peeled, pitted/stoned and thinly sliced
freshly squeezed juice of 1 lemon
4 UK large/US extra-large eggs
freshly ground black pepper

SERVES 2

Preheat the oven to 200°C (400°F) Gas 6.

Stir together the harissa paste and olive oil in a large bowl then toss in the butternut squash and stir again to coat the squash.

Put the butternut squash on a sheet pan with sides and bake in the preheated oven for 30 minutes.

Meanwhile, prepare the avocado and squeeze over the lemon juice to prevent it from turning brown. After 30 minutes, add the olives, tomatoes and avocado to the butternut squash and bake for a further 10 minutes.

Make four wells in the vegetables and crack in the eggs. Bake for another 6–9 minutes until the egg whites are cooked. Season with freshly ground black pepper and serve.

GOATS' CHEESE & VEG STACKS

These colourful and nutrient-rich cheese and vegetable stacks are not only mouth-watering but also really simple to create.

2 medium sweet potatoes, peeled and cut into 1-cm/¹/₂-in. thick discs
2 medium aubergines/eggplants, cut into 2-cm/³/₄-in. thick discs
3 tablespoons olive oil
1¹/₂ teaspoons sea salt
2 beef tomatoes, cut into 2-cm/³/₄-in. thick discs

150 g/5¹/₂ oz. goats' cheese log, cut into 1-cm/¹/₂-in. thick discs
2 teaspoons dried basil
freshly ground black pepper

SERVES 3-4

Preheat the oven to 200°C (400°F) Gas 6.

Lay the sweet potato and aubergine/eggplant discs out on a large sheet pan. Cover in the olive oil (more so on the aubergines/eggplants) and salt and bake in the preheated oven for up to 20 minutes – until they are just cooked.

Once cooked, on the same sheet pan, stack a tomato disc, then the cooked aubergine/eggplant, followed by the cooked sweet potato and finally the goats' cheese.

Bake for another 10 minutes. Sprinkle over the dried basil and freshly ground black pepper and serve.

Serving Suggestion: Serve with a large salad.

COURGETTE CRUST MINI PESTO QUICHES

A light summer supper. These mini quiches are delicious served with a large salad, avocado and coleslaw.

1 courgette/zucchini, very thinly sliced with a mandolin or vegetable peeler (discard the core, it is too wet to use in this recipe)
4 UK large/US extra-large eggs
2 tablespoons green pesto

2 vines of cherry tomatoes

4 x silicone muffin cases, greased, or a muffin pan, greased

SERVES 2

Preheat the oven to 200°C (400°F) Gas 6.

Line the four silicone muffin cases/pan holes, including the base, with one layer of sliced courgette/zucchini. Don't worry if there's some overlap.

Next, whisk together the eggs and pesto in a medium-sized bowl and pour the mixture into the muffin holes.

Bake in the preheated oven for 18–20 minutes until risen and no runny egg remains. Add the tomatoes to the oven 10 minutes before the end of baking (either on the same baking sheet as the muffin cases or a separate sheet if using a muffin pan for the quiches).

Serving Suggestion: Serve the mini quiches and tomatoes together with some sliced avocado and Creamy Coleslaw (page 122).

BAKED HONEY & THYME CAMEMBERT WITH CRUDITÉS

How to make friends and influence people? Serve them this oozing, melted cheese with a selection of colourful chopped vegetables and apple slices.

1 x 250-g/9-oz. Camembert
leaves from 2 sprigs of fresh thyme
2 tablespoons runny honey
1 red (bell) pepper, sliced into
   1-cm/¹/₂-in. pieces
1 Granny Smith apple, cored and sliced into
   8 wedges
1 large carrot, cut into 3-cm/1¹/₄-in. fingers

SERVES 2-4

Preheat the oven to 200°C (400°F) Gas 6.

Score the top of the Camembert with a sharp knife, but leave the cheese in the box.

Push the thyme leaves into the scores, then drizzle over the honey.

Replace the lid, loosely, and place the box on a sheet pan.

Bake the Camembert in the preheated oven for 20 minutes until the cheese is all melted and wobbles when you move the sheet pan gently.

Serve the Camembert with the (bell) pepper, apple and carrot crudités.

Serving Suggestion: Serve with chunks of sourdough bread.

BAKED MEDITERRANEAN FETA

200 g/7 oz. feta, cut into 4 triangles
2 medium vine tomatoes, quartered
   lengthways
¹/₂ courgette/zucchini, thinly sliced with
   a mandolin or peeler
¹/₈ teaspoon dried basil
¹/₈ teaspoon dried marjoram
2 tablespoons olive oil
grated zest and freshly squeezed juice
   of ¹/₂ lemon

SERVES 2

Feta has such a unique flavour and texture it deserves to be the star of the show in this 'dish of its own'. This is a very sociable dish.

Preheat the oven to 180°C (350°F) Gas 4.

Place all of the ingredients into a bowl and mix together using your hands. Tip the ingredients onto a small sheet pan with sides. Bake in the preheated oven for 15 minutes or until the vegetables are cooked. Serve.

Serving Suggestion: Serve with avocado slices and a green salad.

HALLOUMI, QUINOA & VEGETABLE BAKE

Mixing what is now known as a 'pseudo-grain' quinoa, with a flavour-packed combination of vegetables and the unique flavour and texture of halloumi, this is a quick supper and one to be enjoyed whilst hot because that's when soft, melted halloumi is at its finest.

2 medium sweet potatoes, peeled and chopped into 2-cm/^{3}/$_4$-in. dice
1 medium aubergine/eggplant, chopped into 2-cm/^{3}/$_4$-in. dice
2 celery stalks, chopped into 2-cm/^{3}/$_4$-in. lengths
2 tablespoons olive oil
1 x 250-g/9-oz. packet cooked quinoa
250 g/9 oz. passata/strained tomatoes
1 teaspoon dried mixed herbs
250 g/9 oz. halloumi, sliced
sea salt and freshly ground black pepper

SERVES 4

Preheat the oven to 180°C (350°F) Gas 4.

Toss the chopped vegetables in the olive oil, then roast in a sheet pan with sides in the preheated oven for 35–40 minutes until soft.

Stir in the cooked quinoa, passata/strained tomatoes, mixed herbs and salt and pepper. Top with the sliced halloumi and bake for another 10 minutes. If you like the halloumi browned, then simply place it under a preheated hot grill/broiler for 3 minutes at the end. Serve.

Serving Suggestion: Serve with a large green salad.

MANGO & AVOCADO SALSA

This is such a sublime combination of flavours designed to complement some of the main meals in this book.

1 mango, peeled, stoned/pitted and finely chopped
1 avocado, peeled, stoned/pitted and diced
^{1}/$_2$ red onion, finely chopped
1 red chilli/chile, deseeded and finely chopped
2 tablespoons freshly squeezed lime juice
1 tablespoon apple cider vinegar
2 tablespoons olive oil
2 tablespoons freshly chopped mint
sea salt

SERVES 4
AS A SIDE DISH

In a large bowl, combine all the ingredients either by hand or using a spoon. Season with salt to taste.

Cover and allow the flavours to combine for 30 minutes before serving.

ROASTED FIG SALAD

Such a wonderful flavour combination – salty blue cheese and sweet figs. Although this is a light meal it is very satisfying. If the rocket/arugula is too peppery for some, then try a little romaine or Little Gem Lettuce underneath the cheesy baked figs.

4 fresh, ripe figs
40 g/1½ oz. blue cheese, crumbled
90 g/3¼ oz. rocket/arugula leaves
35 g/¼ cup chopped walnuts

for the dressing
1¼ teaspoons olive oil
2 teaspoons balsamic vinegar
¼ teaspoon runny honey
¼ teaspoon wholegrain mustard
sea salt and freshly ground black pepper

SERVES 2

Preheat the oven to 200°C (400°F) Gas 6.

Carefully cut halfway down each fig from the top, in a cross. Push the sides of the fig together so that it opens up slightly and put on a sheet pan with sides.

Crumble the blue cheese into the cross of each fig and bake in the preheated oven for 4 minutes.

Meanwhile, make the dressing by whisking together the ingredients in a bowl or shaking in a jar to combine.

Put some rocket/arugula leaves on two plates and top with two of the figs filled with blue cheese, then drizzle some of the dressing. Scatter over the walnuts and serve.

HONEY HARISSA HALLOUMI BAKE

A summery supper that may make you believe that you are indeed on holiday in sunnier climes. The sweet honey and mild spices contrast deliciously with the salty halloumi cheese. One to be eaten whilst hot, otherwise the cheese can turn a little rubbery as it cools.

2 red onions, sliced into wedges
200 g/7 oz. peeled and deseeded butternut squash, cut into 1-cm/½-in. cubes
1 teaspoon olive oil
½ teaspoon sea salt

1 teaspoon harissa dry spice mix
1 teaspoon runny honey
150 g/5½ oz. halloumi, cut into 1-cm/½-in. cubes

SERVES 2

Preheat the oven to 200°C (400°F) Gas 6.

Put the onion and butternut squash on a sheet pan with sides. Drizzle over the olive oil and sprinkle over the salt.

Bake in the preheated oven for 30 minutes.

Meanwhile, mix together the harissa spice and honey in a small bowl or ramekin.

After the vegetables have been baking for 30 minutes, add the halloumi and the harissa/honey mix to the sheet pan and give everything a good stir. Bake for a further 10 minutes. Serve.

Serving Suggestion: Serve with Mango & Avocado Salsa (page 86).

GRAIN-FREE TOMATO 'SPAGHETTI' BAKE WITH ROQUEFORT

Whilst many have got over their 'spiralizing craze' this dish holds onto the best bit of the phase, which is the fact that spiralized vegetables bake beautifully and quickly, and create a great lower-carb alternative to the classic pasta bake recipe.

175 g/6 oz. courgetti
   (courgette/zucchini thinly sliced using
   a spiralizer or julienne peeler)
175 g/6 oz. butternut squash 'spaghetti'
   (prepared butternut squash sliced using
   a spiralizer or julienne peeler)
1 teaspoon olive oil
1 teaspoon sea salt
2 UK large/US extra large eggs
330 g/11½ oz. tomato pasta sauce
   (recipe below)
12 pitted black olives
75 g/2¾ oz. crumbled Roquefort

for the sauce
1 teaspoon olive oil
1 onion, chopped
1 courgette/zucchini, chopped
¼ teaspoon garlic salt
½ teaspoon sea salt
1 tablespoon tomato purée/paste
1 x 400-g/14-oz. can chopped tomatoes
1 teaspoon dried oregano

SERVES 4

First, to make the sauce, heat the olive oil in a medium-sized saucepan. Add the onion and cook for 5 minutes until it's beginning to become translucent. Add the courgette/zucchini and cook for a further 5 minutes.

Add the garlic salt, salt, tomato purée/paste, chopped tomatoes and oregano. Cook for 10 minutes.

Pour the sauce mixture into a food processor and process to the consistency of a thick tomato sauce. Transfer to a small saucepan and keep at a gentle simmer over a low heat until ready to use.

Preheat the oven to 200°C (400°F) Gas 6.

Put the courgetti and butternut squash 'spaghetti' in a sheet pan or baking dish with sides. Drizzle over the olive oil and sprinkle on the salt. Mix well. Bake in the preheated oven for 10 minutes.

Meanwhile, whisk the eggs in a large bowl and then add the hot pasta sauce and stir.

Remove the vegetable 'spaghetti' from the oven, then pour over the sauce mixture. Any remaining sauce can be kept in the fridge for up to 3 days. Add the olives and crumbled Roquefort before serving. Place the dish under a medium grill/broiler to melt the cheese, if desired, and serve.

VEGAN

PESTO-BAKED MUSHROOMS WITH SUN-DRIED TOMATOES

A delightful summery vegan dish with meltingly soft mushrooms combined with the classic flavours of pesto, tomatoes and capers. Of course, cooked mushrooms provide an 'umami' taste that is ever so satisfying.

4 large flat mushrooms
4 heaped teaspoons vegan pesto
   (recipe below)
3 tablespoons sun-dried tomatoes in
   olive oil, drained
1 tablespoon capers or 2 tablespoons
   black olives
olive oil, for drizzling

SERVES 4
AS A STARTER

Preheat the oven to 180°C (350°F) Gas 4.

Wipe the mushrooms clean and remove the stalks. Spread the pesto onto the underside of the mushrooms with the back of a teaspoon. Place the mushrooms on a sheet pan with sides and bake in the preheated oven for 15 minutes.

Add the capers or olives and sun-dried tomatoes to the sheet pan and cook for a further 7–10 minutes until everything is the same temperature. Remove from the oven and serve.

Serving Suggestion: Serve with Butter Bean Purée with Lemon & Garlic (page 121) and rocket/arugula leaves.

VEGAN PESTO

Pesto is surprisingly simple to prepare and can really elevate a dish.
It's delicious paired with baked mushrooms, courgettes and kale.

40 g/¼ cup sunflower seeds
75 g/5 cups fresh basil leaves
½ garlic clove, peeled
1 teaspoon freshly squeezed lemon juice
5 tablespoons olive oil
sea salt and freshly ground black pepper

To make the pesto, put the sunflower seeds into a food processor and whizz to a powder. Add all the other ingredients (except the oil) and whizz until combined. Finally, add the oil, whizz to mix and check the seasoning. The pesto can be stored in a glass jar with a lid for up to 3 days in the refrigerator.

PESTO SUMMER VEG BAKE

Pesto IS the taste of summer and especially when combined with seasonal vegetables as it is in this perfect summer dish.

2 medium courgettes/zucchini,
    sliced into 3-mm/⅛-in. thick rounds
1 medium aubergine/eggplant,
    sliced into 3-mm/⅛-in. thick rounds
12 cherry tomatoes
4 tablespoons Vegan Pesto (page 95)
4 tablespoons olive oil
1 tablespoon freshly chopped parsley

SERVES 4

Preheat the oven to 180°C (350°F) Gas 4.

Place all of the vegetables in a bowl.

Mix together the pesto and olive oil to create pesto oil. Pour over the vegetables and stir to coat the vegetables.

Lay all the vegetables out on two sheet pans with sides.

Bake the vegetables in the preheated oven for 30 minutes, turning them over from time to time.

Scatter the parsley over the top before serving.

Serving Suggestion: Layer the vegetables together in a serving dish and serve with Butter Bean Purée with Lemon & Garlic (page 121) and a green salad.

VEGETABLE RISOTTO

The joy of not having to stand over the hob stirring constantly and still getting a perfectly textured risotto after 45 minutes baking! There's versatility in this recipe and scope to make it your own by roasting your own vegetables or adding your own leftover vegetables too.

1 red onion, sliced into wedges
    (roughly 8 wedges)
10 mushrooms, cut into quarters
1 red (bell) pepper, deseeded and
    cut into thin slices
1 tablespoon olive oil
¼ teaspoon sea salt
200 g/1 cup Arborio rice
400 ml/1⅔ cups hot vegetable stock
1 tablespoon nutritional yeast flakes
    (optional)
1 tablespoon freshly chopped flat leaf parsley
sea salt and freshly ground black pepper

SERVES 4

Preheat the oven to 200°C (400°F) Gas 6.

Put the vegetables in a medium-sized sheet pan with sides, drizzle over the olive oil and sprinkle over the salt.

Bake in the preheated oven for 15 minutes. Add the rice and stir. Add the vegetable stock, then cover the sheet pan tightly with foil.

Bake in the oven for a further 30 minutes. Stir in the yeast flakes, if using. Season to taste. Scatter the parsley over the top and serve.

Serving Suggestion: Serve with avocado and rocket/arugula salad, drizzled with olive oil and freshly squeezed lemon juice, plus a little black pepper.

SWEET POTATO FALAFEL WITH COURGETTES & PEPPERS

This dish, incorporating flavour-packed falafel with roasted courgettes/zucchini and (bell) peppers is a favourite with all ages from babies, who can enjoy it as finger food, to older folk.

1 courgette/zucchini,
    cut into 2-cm/³/₄-in. thick rounds
1 red (bell) pepper, deseeded and
    cut into 2-cm/³/₄-in. thick strips
2 teaspoons olive oil
sea salt and freshly ground black pepper

for the falafel
400 g/14 oz. cooked sweet potatoes
    (skins removed)
100 g/³/₄ cup canned chickpeas,
    drained and rinsed
50 g/¹/₃ cup gram (chickpea) flour
¹/₂ teaspoon ground coriander
1 teaspoon ground cumin
freshly squeezed juice of ¹/₄ lemon
¹/₂ teaspoon sea salt

SERVES 4

Put all the falafel ingredients into a food processor and whizz to combine to a smooth but thick paste. Transfer to a bowl, cover and leave in the refrigerator for 24 hours.

Preheat the oven to 190°C (375°F) Gas 5.

Remove the falafel mixture from the refrigerator and shape into small falafel quenelles using two spoons.

Put the falafel, courgette/zucchini and (bell) pepper on a sheet pan with sides and sprinkle over the olive oil and seasoning.

Bake in the preheated oven for 25 minutes.

Serve the falafel and baked vegetables together.

SIMPLE THAI VEGETABLES

Thai flavours are so aromatic and exotic-tasting. This is a great dish to make when you're caught short and have very little fresh food in. It requires frozen vegetables and storecupboard ingredients only. It's a saucy one, so enjoy with rice to soak up the sauce. Eat immediately as the sauce tends to separate if left to cool.

5 tablespoons frozen peas
2 large handfuls frozen butternut
   squash pieces
2 handfuls frozen spinach
300 ml/1¼ cups coconut milk
1 teaspoon freshly squeezed lime
   or lemon juice
2½ teaspoons tamari
1 teaspoon coconut sugar
1½ teaspoons dried Thai spice mix
freshly chopped coriander/cilantro
   or Thai basil leaves, to garnish

SERVES 4

Preheat the oven to 200°C (400°F) Gas 6.

Put the frozen peas, butternut squash and spinach in a deep-sided sheet pan.

Put the coconut milk, lime or lemon juice, tamari, coconut sugar and Thai spice mix in a bowl and mix together. Pour the mixture over the vegetables and stir.

Bake in the preheated oven for 30 minutes, stirring twice during baking.

Garnish with the fresh herbs and serve hot with rice.

CHICKPEA & PEPPER CURRY BAKE

5 shallots, very finely chopped

2 small garlic cloves, very finely chopped

2-cm/³/₄-in. piece of fresh ginger,
    peeled and grated

2 teaspoons ground cumin

³/₄ teaspoon ground coriander

1 teaspoon ground turmeric

1 x 400-g/14-oz. can tomatoes

1 x 400-g/14-oz. can coconut milk

2 teaspoons sea salt

¹/₂ yellow (bell) pepper, deseeded and
    thinly sliced

¹/₂ red (bell) pepper, deseeded and
    thinly sliced

¹/₂ orange (bell) pepper, deseeded and
    thinly sliced

2 x 400-g/14-oz. cans chickpeas,
    drained and rinsed

freshly chopped coriander/cilantro, to serve

SERVES 4

Chickpeas and (bell) peppers combine beautifully in this dish to bring sweetness, tanginess and yet the mellowness of a substantial vegan baked meal-in-one.

Preheat the oven to 220°C (425°F) Gas 7.

Mix the shallots, garlic, ginger, spices, tomatoes and coconut milk together in a bowl or food processor.

Put the sliced (bell) peppers on a sheet pan with sides. Pour over the coconut milk and spice mixture. Cover with foil and bake in the preheated oven for 30 minutes.

Add the chickpeas to the curry mix and stir. Bake for another 5 minutes. Sprinkle over the coriander/cilantro and serve with rice.

CHICKPEA & VEGETABLE CURRY BAKE

2 large carrots, cut into 15-mm/⁵/₈-in. cubes

1 cauliflower, cut into small florets

1 teaspoon ground cumin

¹/₄ teaspoon ground turmeric

1¹/₄ teaspoons sea salt

1 tablespoon olive oil

1 red (bell) pepper, deseeded and
    very finely chopped

2 onions, very finely chopped

2 garlic cloves, crushed

1¹/₂ teaspoons grated (peeled) fresh ginger

¹/₂ teaspoon grated (peeled) fresh turmeric

1 tablespoon tomato purée/paste

1 x 160-ml/5¹/₂-oz. can coconut cream

100 ml/¹/₃ cup vegetable stock

1 x 400-g/14-oz. can chickpeas,
    drained and rinsed

50 g/¹/₃ cup cashew nuts

SERVES 4

This is a substantial and colourful family dish combining chickpeas and vegetables. The baking of the dish brings out the flavours of all the ingredients.

Preheat the oven to 200°C (400°F) Gas 6.

Put the carrots and cauliflower on a sheet pan and sprinkle over the ground cumin and turmeric. Next, sprinkle over ³/₄ teaspoon of the salt and drizzle over the olive oil. Bake in the preheated oven for 20 minutes.

In a medium bowl or in a food processor, mix the chopped red (bell) pepper, onions, garlic, ginger and fresh turmeric with the tomato purée/paste, coconut cream and stock, plus the remaining ¹/₂ teaspoon salt.

Pour the sauce over the vegetables, cover the sheet pan tightly in foil and bake for a further 20 minutes.

Check that the sauce is cooked (i.e. that the onions and (bell) pepper taste sweet), remove the foil, stir and add the chickpeas and cashew nuts. Give everything another stir and bake for a further 5 minutes before serving over rice. Alternatively, serve in a bowl with a good dollop of coconut milk yogurt.

BUTTERNUT SQUASH & CAULIFLOWER LENTIL KORMA

This is a very cost-effective and colourful vegan tray bake, combining sweet but not too starchy butternut squash and cauliflower with lentils and spices. This is a mild vegan curry that will tempt reluctant vegans!

2 red onions, cut into quarters
400 g/14 oz. butternut squash, peeled, deseeded and cut into 1-cm/$1/2$-in. cubes
$1/2$ cauliflower, cut into florets
2 teaspoons olive oil
60 g/$1/4$ cup korma curry paste
200 ml/generous $3/4$ cup coconut milk
1 x 400-g/14-oz. can green lentils, drained and rinsed
1 lemon, cut into quarters, to serve
1 tablespoon freshly chopped coriander/ cilantro, to serve

SERVES 2

Preheat the oven to 200°C (400°F) Gas 6.

Put the onions, butternut squash and cauliflower in a sheet pan with sides and drizzle over the olive oil.

Bake in the preheated oven for 30–35 minutes until all the vegetables are soft and the cauliflower is also brown and crispy at the edges.

Meanwhile, mix the curry paste and coconut milk together. Pour the mixture over the vegetables and stir in the lentils.

Bake for a further 10 minutes. Squeeze over the lemon quarters, sprinkle over the coriander/cilantro and serve.

Serving Suggestion: Serve with rice.

VEGAN BAKED FAJITAS

Fajitas seem like the best party food to serve to a crowd. Making up your own fajita whilst sat around a table with your friends or family is such a sociable way to enjoy a meal. In this book, you'll find both meat and vegan fajita dishes so there is something for everyone at party time!

2 medium sweet potatoes, peeled and chopped into 1.5-cm/$^1/_2$-in. pieces
3 teaspoons olive oil
2 (bell) peppers, ideally different colours, deseeded and cut into 2-cm/$^3/_4$-in. long slices
2 red onions, sliced into thin wedges
1 x 28-g/1-oz. packet of fajita seasoning mix (try to avoid those with sugar as the prime ingredient)
1 x 400-g/14-oz. can chickpeas, drained and rinsed

SERVES 4

Preheat the oven to 200°C (400°F) Gas 6.

Put the sweet potatoes on a large sheet pan with sides. Drizzle over $^1/_2$ teaspoon of the olive oil. Bake in the preheated oven for 15 minutes.

Meanwhile, mix the (bell) peppers, onions, remaining 2$^1/_2$ teaspoons olive oil and the fajita seasoning together in a bowl.

Once the sweet potatoes have been baking for 15 minutes, add the (bell) pepper and onion mix to the sheet pan and stir.

Bake for another 15 minutes then add the chickpeas for the last minute and stir well. Serve.

Serving Suggestion: Serve with Avocado Mayonnaise (page 122), coconut yogurt and either wraps or rice.

BALSAMIC TEMPEH & CRISPY CAULIFLOWER

What a treat tempeh is! A naturally-fermented food which means it is more nutritious and easier to digest than modified and processed soy-based foods. This balsamic tempeh is rich in flavour. Just try it and I bet you'll be coming back for more.

2 tablespoons balsamic glaze
¼ teaspoon garlic salt
1 teaspoon maple syrup
2 tablespoons olive oil
1 x 200-g/7-oz. pack tempeh
½ cauliflower, cut into florets
½ teaspoon sea salt

SERVES 2

Preheat the oven to 190°C (375°F) Gas 5.

In a bowl, mix together the balsamic glaze, garlic salt, maple syrup and 1 tablespoon of the olive oil.

Wash the tempeh and pat it dry. Cut it into 16 squares or triangles.

Place the tempeh into the marinade and turn to coat.

Put the cauliflower florets on a sheet pan with sides, sprinkle over the remaining 1 tablespoon olive oil and the salt. Make a space in the middle of the cauliflower for the tempeh. Tip the tempeh and marinade into the sheet pan.

Roast in the preheated oven for 30–35 minutes until the cauliflower is crispy at the edges and the marinade mostly absorbed. Serve immediately.

ROASTED SUMMER VEGETABLES

A Mediterranean mix of vegetables and flavours. This dish would be complemented by some avocado slices with lemon juice and black pepper and some hummus.

1 red onion, halved and finely sliced
4 medium mushrooms, thinly sliced
10 cherry tomatoes, halved
1/2 courgette/zucchini, thinly sliced using a mandolin
2 teaspoons olive oil
1/2 teaspoon sea salt
freshly squeezed juice of 1/4 lemon
1 tablespoon fresh basil leaves

SERVES 2

Preheat the oven to 200°C (400°F) Gas 6.

Put all of the vegetables on a sheet pan with sides. Drizzle over the olive oil, then sprinkle over the salt.

Bake in the preheated oven for 20 minutes. Stir once during baking.

When you are ready to serve, squeeze over the lemon juice and sprinkle over the chopped basil.

Serving Suggestion: Serve with avocado slices, hummus and lemon wedges.

ROASTED MISO AUBERGINE

Miso is another fermented soy food which means it's easier for our bodies to digest. It has such a rich flavour, that combined with the soft, melting flavour and texture of aubergines makes for a very exciting Asian-themed tray bake.

1 medium aubergine/eggplant (or 2 if they're small)
1 1/2 tablespoons olive oil
1 tablespoon miso paste
1 teaspoon runny honey or maple syrup
1 tablespoon tamari
1 tablespoon hot water
2-cm/1/2-in. piece of fresh ginger, peeled and grated
1 garlic clove, crushed
4 spring onions/scallions, thinly sliced on the diagonal

SERVES 2

Preheat the oven to 200°C (400°F) Gas 6.

Slice the aubergine/eggplant in half lengthways. Score the flesh in a diamond pattern, being careful not to pierce the skin. Place on a sheet pan, skin-side down. Pour over the olive oil and bake in the preheated oven for 20 minutes.

Meanwhile, combine the miso, honey, tamari, water, ginger and garlic in a bowl.

After 20 minutes, check the aubergine/eggplant is well on its way to being cooked. Coat the flesh of the aubergine/eggplant with the miso paste/tamari mix and bake for a further 10 minutes until the aubergine/eggplant is cooked.

Serve with the sliced spring onions/scallions scattered over the top.

RATATOUILLE BAKED BEANS

1 medium aubergine/eggplant,
   cut into 2-cm/³/₄-in. cubes
1 red (bell) pepper, deseeded and
   cut into 2-cm/³/₄-in. pieces
¼ large butternut squash, deseeded,
   peeled and cut into 2-cm/³/₄-in. cubes
1 onion, cut into 8 wedges
1 tablespoon olive oil
1 teaspoon sea salt
1 x 400-g/14-oz. can cannellini beans,
   drained and rinsed
12 stoned/pitted black olives, halved
1 x 400-g/14-oz. can chopped tomatoes
2 tablespoons tomato purée/paste
1 teaspoon maple syrup
1½ teaspoons freshly chopped basil leaves

SERVES 4

A combination of two classics – ratatouille and baked beans – this dish is delightfully flavoursome. This is an ideal celebratory vegan meal to enjoy with friends or family.

Preheat the oven to 200°C (400°F) Gas 6.

Place the chopped aubergine/eggplant, (bell) pepper, squash and onion on a sheet pan with sides.

Drizzle over the olive oil and sprinkle over the salt. Bake in the preheated oven for 30 minutes until the vegetables are soft.

Add the cannellini beans, black olives, chopped tomatoes, tomato purée/paste and maple syrup and stir. Bake for a further 10 minutes. Serve with the basil scattered over the top.

Serving Suggestion: Serve with crushed new potatoes.

BLACK BEAN & SWEET POTATO CHILLI

2 large sweet potatoes, peeled and
   cut into 2-cm/³/₄-in. pieces
1 teaspoon coconut or olive oil
1 teaspoon sea salt
2 red onions, cut into 6 wedges
1 red (bell) pepper, halved, deseeded and
   sliced into 1-cm/¹/₂-in. thick lengths
1 x 500-g/17-oz. carton passata/strained
   tomatoes
³/₄ teaspoon smoked paprika
¹/₂ teaspoon ground cumin
³/₄ teaspoon dried marjoram
¹/₈ teaspoon chilli/chili powder
¹/₈ teaspoon ground cinnamon
1 x 400-g/14-oz. can black beans,
   drained and rinsed

SERVES 6

This dish provides a rich combination of sweet potatoes with tangy tomatoes and soft, smooth and satisfying black beans. It's a colourful combination and ideal for a vegan feast of any proportion.

Preheat the oven to 200°C (400°F) Gas 6.

Put the sweet potatoes in a sheet pan with sides. Drizzle over the melted coconut oil or olive oil and sprinkle over ¹/₄ teaspoon of the salt.

Bake in the preheated oven for 10 minutes. Add the onions and red (bell) pepper and bake for a further 20 minutes, stirring once during baking.

Next, mix together the passata/strained tomatoes, paprika, cumin, marjoram, chilli/chili powder, cinnamon and the remaining ³/₄ teaspoon salt.

After the vegetables have been baking for 30 minutes, add the black beans to the sheet pan, stir, then add the passata/strained tomatoes and spice mix. Stir this well too. Bake for a further 15 minutes, then serve.

SIDES & SALADS

TWICE-BAKED CHEESY POTATOES

These potatoes are almost a meal in themselves and are delicious alongside a crisp salad and fresh tomatoes. Alternatively, enjoy a half filled potato as your carbohydrate portion in your main meal.

2 large baking potatoes
40 g/^{1}/$_3$ cup grated/shredded
    Cheddar cheese
60 g/^{1}/$_4$ cup soured cream
^{1}/$_2$ teaspoon sea salt

SERVES 4
AS A SIDE DISH

Preheat the oven to 220°C (425°F) Gas 7.

Pierce the baking potatoes lightly with a fork. Put the potatoes on the middle shelf of the preheated oven and bake for 45 minutes until tender.

Remove the potatoes from the oven and carefully slice in half. Scoop out the insides of the potatoes using a blunt knife or spoon, being careful not to slit the skin.

Mash the potato flesh with the grated/shredded cheese until the cheese is all melted, then mash in the soured cream and salt.

Put the potato skins on a sheet pan and fill the skins with the cheesy mash.

Bake for a further 15 minutes. Serve immediately.

PERFECT ROAST POTATOES

Who doesn't love a perfectly roasted potato? I'll admit that it took me a while and a consultation with my mother before reaching a method of producing perfectly roasted potatoes that I was happy with. This is the result.

2.5 kg/5^1/$_2$ lb. potatoes, such as Maris Piper,
    peeled and quartered lengthways
5 tablespoons goose or duck fat
sea salt and freshly ground black pepper

SERVES 6
AS A SIDE DISH

Preheat the oven to 200°C (400°F) Gas 6.

Put the potatoes in a large saucepan, cover with water and add a little salt. Bring to the boil, then simmer for 8 minutes. Drain really well, tossing in a colander so all surfaces of the potatoes dry.

On the hob, heat the goose or duck fat in a sheet pan with sides (not one with a non-stick coating). Toss the potatoes in the fat. Season well with salt and pepper.

Continue cooking on the hob and once all surfaces of the potatoes are starting to brown put the potatoes in the preheated oven and roast for 40 minutes or until crispy. Serve.

QUINOA TABBOULEH

Of course traditional tabbouleh is made with bulgur wheat. I prefer using pseudo-grains or no grains over grains and this is no exception for reasons of nutrition and easier digestion. The quinoa works really well in this straightforward dish.

150 g/³⁄₄ cup quinoa
4 vine-ripened tomatoes, peeled, deseeded and diced
2–3 tablespoons freshly chopped flat leaf parsley
2–3 tablespoons freshly chopped mint
¹⁄₂ red onion, very thinly sliced (optional)
6 spring onions/scallions, finely sliced

for the dressing
6 tablespoons extra virgin olive oil
freshly squeezed juice of 2 lemons
sea salt and freshly ground black pepper

SERVES 6

Place the quinoa in a sieve/strainer and rinse thoroughly. Put into a saucepan with 250 ml/1 cup of water.

Bring to the boil, then turn down the heat. Cover and leave to simmer for 15–20 minutes until the quinoa is tender and the water is absorbed. Transfer to a bowl and leave to cool.

Add the diced tomatoes to the quinoa, then stir in the parsley, mint, red onion (if using) and spring onions/scallions.

Whisk together all the ingredients for the dressing in a small bowl and season to taste. Pour over the tabbouleh. Stir, then serve.

EGG-FRIED CAULIFLOWER RICE

A very useful side dish for so many meals. Cauliflower rice is super absorbent so it works well with saucy tray bakes. This version with egg boosts the protein and nutrient content even further. It's a great match for saucy Asian bakes.

175 g/6 oz. cauliflower florets
1 tablespoon olive oil
2¹⁄₂ tablespoons frozen peas
¹⁄₈ teaspoon fish sauce
¹⁄₄ teaspoon tamari
1 UK large/US extra large egg, beaten
2 spring onions/scallions, thinly sliced on the diagonal

SERVES 2
AS A SIDE DISH

Pulse the cauliflower in a food processor until it becomes a rice-like consistency.

Heat the olive oil in a small frying pan/skillet over a low-medium heat and add the cauliflower rice. Stir for about 6 minutes, then add the frozen peas, fish sauce and tamari.

Stir until everything is heated through (about 2 minutes), then add the beaten egg.

Immediately remove from the heat and stir for about 1 minute, making sure the egg is cooked through. It should take on a slightly 'scrambled' consistency.

Serve with the sliced spring onions/scallions scattered on top.

CUMIN-ROASTED CHICKPEAS

These make a fantastic topping to a meal or salad. They work really well with many of the Asian-inspired tray bakes in this book.

1 x 400-g/14-oz. can chickpeas, drained and rinsed
1 teaspoon garlic powder
1 teaspoon onion powder
1/2 teaspoon ground cumin
1 tablespoon olive oil
1/4–1/2 teaspoon sea salt

SERVES 2
AS A SIDE DISH

Preheat the oven to 200°C (400°F) Gas 6.

In a bowl, toss the chickpeas in the garlic powder, onion powder, cumin and olive oil.

Put the chickpeas on a sheet pan with sides. Bake in the preheated oven for 30 minutes until lightly toasted. Shake the pan a couple of times during the baking time to ensure the chickpeas cook evenly.

Remove from the oven. Sprinkle over the salt to taste. Serve hot or cold. If serving cold, allow to cool then store in an airtight container until ready to be consumed. They are best eaten within 24 hours.

BUTTER BEAN PURÉE WITH LEMON & GARLIC

A protein-rich alternative to mashed potato, this purée works wonderfully well with tomato-based tray bakes.

1 x 400-g/14-oz. can butter beans, drained and rinsed
1 small garlic clove, thinly sliced
2 tablespoons olive oil
freshly squeezed juice of 1 lemon
sea salt and freshly ground black pepper

SERVES 2
AS A SIDE DISH

Put the butter beans and garlic in a small saucepan, add enough water to cover and bring to a simmer, then drain.

Put the beans and garlic in a food processor. Add the olive oil, then the lemon juice whilst the blade is moving until you have a thin mashed potato consistency. Season to taste with salt and pepper. Serve warm or cold.

CITRUS FENNEL SALAD

This delightfully light salad will remind you just how delicious fennel can be.

2 tablespoons extra virgin olive oil
1 tablespoon apple cider vinegar
freshly squeezed juice of 1/2 lemon
4 fennel bulbs, grated
sea salt

SERVES 6

Whisk the olive oil, apple cider vinegar and lemon juice together in a large bowl.

Add the grated fennel and stir.

Season to taste with salt, stir and serve.

CREAMY COLESLAW

This delicious coleslaw can be whipped up in minutes. A combination of mayonnaise, soured cream and a variety of condiments, it is an ideal partner to many of the more substantial meals in this book.

1/2 white cabbage, thinly sliced
2 medium carrots, grated
1 red onion, thinly sliced
75 g/2³/4 oz. mayonnaise
1 tablespoon soured cream
1 tablespoon apple cider vinegar
1 tablespoon mustard powder
1 tablespoon coconut sugar
sea salt and freshly ground black pepper

SERVES 6

First prepare the vegetables and mix them together in a large bowl.

Put the mayonnaise, soured cream, vinegar, mustard powder, coconut sugar and salt and pepper in a small bowl and mix together.

Stir the mayonnaise mixture into the prepared vegetables. Cover and leave to mellow in the fridge for a few hours before serving.

AVOCADO MAYONNAISE

This was an accidental discovery whilst trying to use up avocados. It's an excellent match for burgers.

3 ripe avocados, pitted/stoned
  and skin removed
1 tablespoon freshly squeezed
  lemon juice
1 tablespoon apple cider vinegar
2 tablespoons olive oil
sea salt and freshly ground black pepper

SERVES 6

Put all the ingredients, except the olive oil, into a food processor and process to a paste.

Add the olive oil and process again. Adjust the lemon juice, vinegar and salt and pepper to your preferred taste. Serve.

SIMPLE SALAD WITH DRESSING

This is a simple side salad with a straightforward dressing made from storecupboard ingredients.
It works well with many of the main meals in this book.

1 bag mixed salad leaves
1/2 cucumber, thinly sliced
20 cherry tomatoes, halved
1 red onion, thinly sliced (optional)

for the dressing
2 teaspoons olive oil
1 1/2 tablespoons balsamic vinegar
1 1/2 teaspoons runny honey
1/2 teaspoon wholegrain mustard
sea salt and freshly ground black pepper

SERVES 4
AS A SIDE DISH

Put the salad ingredients into a large bowl.

Mix or whisk together the dressing ingredients. A quick and easy way to do this is to put all the ingredients into a clean bottle or jam jar with a lid and shake until the fat and vinegar have emulsified.

Pour the dressing over the salad and toss the salad components to ensure the dressing is evenly distributed.

Serve the salad immediately.

AUBERGINE PURÉE

Aubergine/eggplant has such a rich, succulent texture when roasted with olive oil. This purée recipe shows aubergine/eggplant off at its best. This is an excellent side dish, especially where the main dish has an Asian theme.

1 large aubergine/eggplant, cut into
   2-cm/3/4-in. cubes
4 tablespoons olive oil
1 tablespoon freshly squeezed lemon juice
1/2 garlic clove, crushed
1/2 teaspoon sea salt
1/4 teaspoon ground cumin

SERVES 4
AS A SIDE DISH

Preheat the oven to 200°C (400°F) Gas 6.

In a large bowl, toss the aubergine/eggplant in 2 tablespoons of the olive oil.

Place on a sheet pan with sides and bake in the preheated oven until soft. This should take about 20 minutes.

Once cooked, remove from the oven, then whizz the cooked aubergine/eggplant with all the other ingredients and the remaining olive oil in a food processor until smooth. Serve hot or cold as a side dish.

SWEET THINGS

GRAIN-FREE GRANOLA

Granola gets a bad name for being full of sugar. This granola uses natural sugars and even forgoes the grains to make it more filling. This means that you need less of it and you can layer it with yogurt for a delicious and rather visually impressive dessert, especially if served in glasses or glass pots.

50 g/5 tablespoons coconut oil, melted
65 g/¼ cup maple syrup
100 g/2 cups dried coconut chips or flakes
100 g/1 cup chopped nuts and/or seeds
½ teaspoon ground cinnamon
a handful of dried fruit

SERVES 3

Preheat the oven to 190°C (375°F) Gas 5.

Mix the melted coconut oil and maple syrup together in a small bowl.

Put the coconut chips or flakes, nuts/seeds, cinnamon and dried fruit in a large bowl and mix together. Pour the coconut oil/maple syrup mixture over the dry ingredients and mix well.

Spread the granola out over a sheet pan lined with baking parchment. Bake in the preheated oven for 15–20 minutes until starting to brown, stirring twice during cooking time. Keep a close eye on it, as it will burn easily. Remove from the oven and leave to cool before serving.

ROASTED PINEAPPLE

Succulent and sweet roasted pineapple really goes down a storm. It's ideal served straight from the oven, and after a meal it works well digestively. A little known fact is that pineapple contains bromelain which is a digestive enzyme.

1 medium pineapple, peeled, cored and
    chopped into 1-cm/½-in. cubes
1 tablespoon coconut sugar
1 tablespoon coconut oil, melted
½ teaspoon ground cinnamon

SERVES 4

Preheat the oven to 220°C (425°F) Gas 7.

Put all the ingredients on a sheet pan with sides and mix together.

Bake in the preheated oven for 15 minutes until caramelized and soft.

Serving Suggestion: Serve hot with whipped cream, crème fraîche or coconut cream.

BANANA BUTTER FLAPJACKS

A flapjack is a tray-baked bar or square made from oats, butter and sugar. This flapjack, however, uses the natural sugars of bananas and honey to sweeten and moisten the bar in place of refined sugar. This is a substantial dessert and one square should suffice, but then you never know.

300 g/10½ oz. ripe peeled bananas, mashed
65 g/4 tablespoons melted butter
40 g/1½ oz. runny honey
1 teaspoon ground cinnamon
225 g/1½ cups rolled oats
20 x 20-cm/8 x 8-in. sheet pan with sides, greased

SERVES 9

Preheat the oven to 200°C (400°F) Gas 6.

Mix all of the ingredients together in a large bowl.

Press the mixture evenly over the base of the prepared sheet pan.

Bake in the preheated oven for 20 minutes until golden brown. Remove from the oven and score nine portions.

Once cooled in the pan, cut into nine portions, remove and serve.

BAKED CHOCOLATE BANANAS

This dessert may be reminiscent of childhood campfires, and if that's what it recalls for you then I'm glad because those life moments are special and dear. It's a winning combination this one. Bananas and chocolate were made for each other.

4 bananas, peeled
1 small packet dark chocolate buttons (you need about 5 buttons for each banana)
½ teaspoon ground cinnamon

SERVES 4

Preheat the oven to 200°C (400°F) Gas 6.

Lay each banana on its side on an individual piece of foil. Slice along the curve of the banana along the top, but only to halfway through the banana. Put chocolate buttons all the way along the slit. Sprinkle ⅛ teaspoon of the cinnamon over the banana. Wrap the banana in the foil parcel.

Place the banana parcels on a sheet pan. Bake in the preheated oven for 15–20 minutes until the banana is soft and the chocolate melted.

BAKED NECTARINES

The sweet, jamminess of these melt-in-the-mouth baked nectarines is such a treat. They're delicious served as a simple dinner-party dessert because they take very little preparation time and taste so impressive.

50 g/3 tablespoons runny honey
½ teaspoon ground cinnamon
¼ teaspoon vanilla extract
4 ripe nectarines, halved and stoned

SERVES 4

Preheat the oven to 200°C (400°F) Gas 6.

Mix together the honey, cinnamon and vanilla extract in a small bowl or ramekin.

Put the nectarines on a sheet pan with sides with the cut-sides side up. Drizzle the honey mixture evenly over the nectarines.

Bake the nectarines into the preheated oven for 20 minutes until soft and jammy but not breaking up.

Serving Suggestion: Serve with natural yogurt or coconut milk yogurt, sprinkled with extra cinnamon.

BAKED CINNAMON PLANTAIN

Plantains have been used in Asian cooking culture for centuries. They can be used in both savoury and sweet dishes, but unlike their cousin the banana, they must be cooked. This dish gives so much flavour from so few ingredients. Don't be put off by trying a new or unfamiliar ingredient. Once you try this, a whole range of options may open up as plantains are so versatile.

1 ripe plantain, peeled and sliced on the diagonal about 2-cm/¾-in. thick
1½ teaspoons coconut oil, melted
½ teaspoon ground cinnamon

SERVES 2

Preheat the oven to 180°C (350°F) Gas 4.

In a bowl, toss the sliced plantain in the melted coconut oil.

Spread out the plantain slices on a small sheet pan with sides and scatter over the ground cinnamon.

Bake in the preheated oven for 10 minutes until the plantain slices appear caramelized.

Serving Suggestion: Serve with yogurt or coconut cream.

BAKED CINNAMON PEARS

Baking pears brings out all of their best qualities. In this case, combining the pears with cinnamon makes them even more delicious. A simple but impressive dessert!

4 ripe pears, quartered and cored
1 tablespoon coconut sugar
1 tablespoon ground cinnamon
2 teaspoons coconut oil

SERVES 4

Preheat the oven to 180°C (350°F) Gas 4.

Place the four quarters of each pear on a piece of foil large enough to wrap around all four pieces.

Mix together the sugar and cinnamon and sprinkle over the pears. Then dab on little pieces of coconut oil or drizzle over if it is liquid – about $1/2$ teaspoon for each pear. Wrap the pear quarters in the foil packages and place on a sheet pan.

Bake in the preheated oven for 30 minutes until soft and glistening. Serve with the juices drizzled over the top.

Serving Suggestion: Serve with coconut yogurt or thick Greek yogurt.

OATEN APPLE CRISP

for the apple base
4 large Bramley apples, peeled, cored and chopped into 1.5-cm/$1/2$-in. cubes
1 tablespoon arrowroot powder
$1/2$ teaspoon ground cinnamon
$1/4$ teaspoon stevia powder
$1/4$ teaspoon ground ginger
a pinch of ground allspice

for the crumble
110 g/$1 1/4$ cups flaked/slivered almonds
30 g/$1/3$ cup ground almonds
100 g/1 cup gluten free rolled oats
60 g/$1/4$ cup maple syrup
60 g/4 tablespoons ghee or melted coconut oil
$3/4$ teaspoon ground cinnamon
a pinch of sea salt

20 x 30-cm/8 x 12-in. sheet pan with sides

SERVES 8

This is a lighter version of an apple crumble. With a deep apple base and a crunchy oat and almond topping, it's an ideal way to end a meal.

Preheat the oven to 220°C (425°F) Gas 7.

First make the apple base. In a large bowl, toss the apples in the arrowroot, cinnamon, stevia, ginger and allspice. Put the apples into the sheet pan.

Next mix together all the crumble ingredients until combined. Spoon the crumble topping all over the apples.

Bake in the preheated oven for 20 minutes, then reduce the temperature to 200°C (400°F) Gas 6 and bake for a further 15 minutes until the top is browned and the cooked apple is bubbling up a little.

Remove from the oven and serve hot or cold.

ORANGE-BAKED RHUBARB

Rhubarb has a finite season so make the most of it whilst it is around. Rhubarb and orange are delightful together and make for a fine dessert. This dessert works exceedingly well with something creamy alongside, such as coconut milk yogurt, coconut cream or cream.

400 g/14 oz. rhubarb, rinsed and cut into 5-cm/2-in. pieces
freshly squeezed zest and juice of 1 orange
1½ tablespoons honey

SERVES 4

Preheat the oven to 180°C (350°F) Gas 4.

Put the rhubarb on a sheet pan with sides.

Squeeze over the orange juice and add the zest, then drizzle over the honey and stir everything together.

Bake in the preheated oven for 30 minutes until the rhubarb is soft. Stir once or twice during baking time.

Serving Suggestion: Serve with natural yogurt, coconut cream or cream.

BAKED ALLSPICE APPLES

In season, a baked apple really does feel like autumn to our family. A delicious combination of apple and ground allspice combine in this dish to create a very cost-effective dessert.

2 Bramley apples
1 tablespoon honey
½ teaspoon ground allspice
1 heaped teaspoon butter or ghee
2 teaspoons almond or peanut butter, to serve

SERVES 2

Preheat the oven to 180°C (350°F) Gas 4.

Core the apples, but leave the bases intact to keep in the filling during cooking. Place the apples on a sheet pan with sides.

Mix the honey, allspice and butter or ghee in a bowl.

Distribute the mixture evenly between the centres of the two apples. Bake in the preheated oven for 25 minutes until the apples are soft. Serve with the nut butter.

STICKY GINGER CAKE

This is a deliciously moist cake that takes me back to my childhood. According to my own children, this cake is 'the taste of Christmas'.

8 ready-to-eat dried dates
20 ready-to-eat dried prunes
75 g/1/4 cup molasses or black treacle
100 g/1/3 cup maple syrup
185 g/3/4 cup natural yogurt or use coconut
   yogurt for a dairy-free version
250 ml/1 cup milk (use coconut milk
   for a dairy-free version)
3 1/2 tablespoons olive oil,
   plus a little extra for greasing
2 eggs, beaten
350 g/2 1/2 cups spelt flour (or for a
   gluten-free version use 170 g/1 1/4 cups
   buckwheat flour, 100 g/3/4 cup brown rice
   flour, 50 g/1/3 cup tapioca starch,
   40 g/1 1/2 oz. ground flaxseeds/linseeds)
2 1/2 teaspoons ground ginger
2 teaspoons ground cinnamon
1 teaspoon bicarbonate of soda/baking soda*
1 teaspoon baking powder*
* use gluten-free versions if looking to make
   a gluten-free cake
27 x 20-cm/10 3/4 x 8-in. brownie pan,
   greased and lined with baking parchment

SERVES 15

Preheat the oven to 180°C (350°F) Gas 4.

Put the dates and prunes into a food processor and process to a paste.

Add the molasses or treacle, maple syrup, yogurt, milk, olive oil and eggs and process again.

In a separate bowl, combine all the dry ingredients.

Mix the dry ingredients in with the wet ingredients to combine.

Pour into the prepared brownie pan.

Bake in the preheated oven for 30 minutes or until a cocktail stick/toothpick inserted into the middle comes out clean.

Remove from the oven and leave to cool a little before slicing into 15 squares before serving. Any leftover portions can be stored in an airtight container for a couple of days in a cool dry place.

APPLE & BLACKBERRY ALMOND CRUMBLE

Almonds in many forms make a fantastic, more easily digested alternative to grain-based flours for many. They also provide great flavour and texture to dishes such as this delightful crumble.

150 g/1 cup fresh blackberries
1 eating apple, cored, cut into wedges, then very thinly sliced
1/8 teaspoon stevia powder
1/4 teaspoon ground cinnamon
65 g/1/2 cup ground almonds
35 g/1/2 cup flaked/slivered almonds
45 g/3 tablespoons ghee or coconut oil
450-g/1-lb. loaf pan or small baking dish

SERVES 2

Preheat the oven to 200°C (400°F) Gas 6.

Put the blackberries and apple slices in the base of the loaf pan.

In a medium bowl, mix together the stevia, cinnamon, ground and flaked almonds and ghee or coconut oil using a spoon or your fingertips.

Tip the crumble mixture over the fruit in an even layer.

Bake in the preheated oven for 25 minutes. Serve.

Serving Suggestion: Serve with coconut cream or cream.

BAKED RICE PUDDING

Rice is such a diverse grain. It lends itself to a variety of dishes including desserts. This rice pudding is a low-sugar, dairy-free dessert made from leftover cooked rice. So not only does it taste great it also means you can use up your leftovers too.

430 g/3 cups cold cooked rice
50 g/1/3 cup raisins
2 eggs, beaten
360 ml/scant 1 1/2 cups almond or coconut milk
85 g/3 oz. unsweetened apple purée
1 teaspoon vanilla bean paste
2 tablespoons maple syrup
1 teaspoon ground cinnamon

20 x 20-cm/8 x 8-in. sheet pan with sides, greased with butter

SERVES 9

Preheat the oven to 200°C (400°F) Gas 6.

Put the cooked rice into the sheet pan and break up with a fork. Sprinkle the raisins evenly over the top.

In a separate bowl, mix together the beaten eggs, milk, apple purée, vanilla and maple syrup. Pour the mixture over the cooked rice and raisins.

Sprinkle the cinnamon evenly over the top.

Bake in the preheated oven for 30 minutes. Eat hot or cold.

Serving Suggestion: Serve with coconut yogurt or Greek yogurt and fresh fruit.

INDEX

ACKNOWLEDGMENTS

Firstly, thank you to all those very loyal followers of Lunchboxdoctor.com who over the years have asked again and again for a recipe book. Finally, here it is! A huge thank you must go to Werner, Amalie and Samuel who have had their palate broadened and their critiquing skills well exercised. They've been an incredible support.

To all my recipe testers, Jo Colley Keyes, Jo Massey, Kate Evans, Shirley Briars, Deepa Mer, Kate Smyth, Susan Vaughan, Claire Foss, Deirdre Swede, Helen Macklin, Catherine Pohl, Anne Loder, Andy Loder, June Bailey and Sarah Clarke, thank you for your patience and willing. I really couldn't have done this without you.

Of course this book would not have been possible without the support and belief of my incredible literary agent, Jane Graham-Maw, and the publisher, Ryland Peters & Small, who only batted a few eyelids when I walked back into their offices 5 years after our initial meeting to talk about a book deal. Just goes to show that if you do what you love and you love what you do then persistence pays off.

I wish to thank the photographer and prop stylist, Steve Painter and the food stylist, Lucy McKelvie for bringing the recipes to life.

Finally, to all my family and friends for their support in encouraging me to follow this path.